A Kick In The Attitude™

13 Kick'n Lessons to Re-Energize Your Attitude for Personal & Professional Success

Sam Glenn
The Authority on Attitude ™
Website: EverythingAttitude.com

TABLE OF CONTENTS:

A Kick in the Attitude

Here is Where the "Kick" Starts

(Read the following affirmation to yourself):

A Great Attitude is a choice.

It is my choice! Nobody can choose it for me.

I will not abandon my attitude to Chance.

The attitude I choose to use when engaging with life will determine my performance, my experiences and what I attract into my life…

It will determine…

Where I go,

What I achieve,

and Who I become.

I always have the choice to make my life better or worse, so…

What choice can I make right now to make my life better?

Life gets better when I get better, and it all starts with my attitude.

*If I desire better experiences
for my life, I must choose
a better attitude.*

*My attitude is the
starting point to…*

…Better relationships

…Overcoming setbacks

…Achieving my dreams, and

*…Getting the best out
of life and myself.*

Introduction:

Another Book on Attitude?

Does having a positive attitude really matter? Does a better attitude actually improve business, relationships or the quality of life? Sure it does! But, if we all know that, why doesn't everyone have and use all the power that comes with having a great attitude?

I am often asked, "Sam, you are one of the foremost experts on the topic of attitude, so do you always have a good attitude?" And the answer is, no, my attitude isn't always automatically all rosy – it takes work. But I am 100% convinced that the work is crucial to my life, health, and success, so I do it. Just know that to live the life I lead, sometimes I have to remind myself of the very things you are about to read. It doesn't happen without effort, but it is well worth it.

For years, even before becoming a speaker and author, I jotted down notes, ideas, stories, favorite quotes and experiences offering tangible insights that I could use to add value to my life, business and relationships.

As I sifted through years and years of notes, I made a discovery – one that I am going to share with you in this book – and one that I believe will enrich the quality of your life in ways you never imagined. The topic of attitude is as old as time, and isn't going anywhere anytime soon. What makes this book different than others on attitude is that I am going to bring the topic to life for you by showing you the different faces to your attitude, and how you can make them work wonders. You're going to uncover the subtle layers between the simple definitions of positive or negative. You will capture the forms that work for you, learning how to put them into action and reap many rewards for your life.

I put this theory to the test years ago when I found myself penniless and without a home to call my own. My attitude was at an all-time low, and I didn't think I had a prayer to get out of the hole I was in. I remember at one point thinking I was doomed, which is an awful feeling to live with. When you are facing desperate times, it can be difficult to determine what choice to make first. But I stumbled upon the realization that the best first choice is to change your attitude. When you do this, everything in you and around you begins to change, including your feelings, energy level, responses, outlook and perspectives. It's quite remarkable how one consistent choice in the direction of improving your attitude can transform your life.

Don't be fooled by the use of "simple." I didn't just say to myself, "Sam, get positive! Be positive!" That doesn't work. Trust me; I have tried it a gazillion times! I did something different, something that would sustain a better attitude, and eventually would surface my best attitude. That is, I discovered that by changing my thoughts, beliefs, and habits, I could transform my entire attitude from negative to positive, thereby changing my life. I also discovered that this process was not unique to me, but would work for anyone. In changing the nature of the way we think and act, we build an attitude force so strong that it will attract favor into our existence. And when I refer to favor, I mean opportunities, the right people, dreams, or whatever we desire. You may have heard of the law of attraction, which comes into play here. The quality of our attitude will determine what we attract and pull into our lives.

I wasn't thankful for my challenging situations years ago. I don't think any of us are when we are going through them. But they put me in a classroom that taught me what I am about to share with you. The way I responded to my obstacles then is what has qualified me to share the insights you are about to be introduced to.

I plan to take you through the huge doorway of attitude, and down the hallways to begin to understand all of its true forms. You will see that attitude can take on many shapes which can hurt us, or stop us from receiving life's rewards. You will also see that it can be used to benefit us beyond belief.

For example, our attitude may take on the expression of humor, or on the other hand, hatred. Humor breaks down barriers, and attracts relationships, health, and success. Hatred causes people and reward to head the other way.

The positive or negative aspect of attitude always exists, but the more subtle and diverse forms that our attitude takes on are the real essence of what attitude has come to mean to me. Depending on which trait or form we choose to use in our interaction with life, our attitude can bless us, or destroy us. That's the power of our attitude!

My goal in sharing this book with you is to deepen your awareness of how dynamic your attitude is, what it can and cannot do for you, and why it is so significant to every aspect of your life. My focus for you is to stretch yourself to do more than simply try to be positive; I would like you to experience life through a "superstar attitude." Once you taste life through this attitude, you will never want to go back. It's like sitting in first class on an airplane: do it once and you won't ever want to fly coach again. It's a whole different life experience. It's one that you will want to have over and over again.

I also intend for this book to provide you with a huge source of encouragement and inspiration, stirring your greatness, igniting your passion, and connecting you with your deepest potential, all while unlocking your creative mind to dream, believe and reflect on what's most meaningful for you. It's not only here to provide a kick in your attitude from the outside; it's about putting a positive kick into your attitude, so that your attitude can guide and reward you from the inside out.

My definition of putting a "kick" into your attitude is strengthening and fine-tuning each aspect of your attitude so that it impacts your life in overwhelmingly positive ways. It is my hope that you will recognize and utilize enthusiasm, determination, perseverance, creativity, patience, courage and a sense of humor. In doing so, you will find and experience value and comfort as you engage in the little and big choices you make.

As you read, your mind may be tempted to stray in different directions. The fast-paced life and responsibilities we carry can cause us to lose focus. So if your mind strays on the worries you have, the bills you need to pay, why that person cut you off today, the calls you have to make, the to-do list, just know that all of that stuff will be waiting for you when you put this book down. This book will help you tackle your concerns and chores with more energy, peace, and productivity. So relax and choose to let it all go for the moment. Take in a nice, deep breath, and allow yourself to embrace the experience that these pages are ready to create for you. Stop every now and then to reflect on your life, because this is all about you. Think about where you are in life, where you want to go, and how you need to get there. Jot down your own ideas and notes. When you put this book down and go back to your daily activities, I want you to feel energized and empowered.

I understand that you have a lot going on, so as you read this book, do so in small chunks. Let it soak in. Keep it near and read it when you can – while in the bathroom, or waiting room, or on the airplane; at bedtime, breakfast, or lunch; or whenever you are able. Make reading this book a life-changing, life-enriching and enjoyable experience.

You will also notice at the end of each chapter is something called an Attitude Kicker. What is this? An Attitude Kicker is someone who is passionate, connected, engaged, and applies the power of attitude in serving customers, overcoming daily challenges, and working effectively at the highest level. Our sections are designed to get your brain working to think of ways that you can become a real life Attitude Kicker. They are small tips or ideas that can be read quickly to make a big difference. So even if you don't have time to read a lot on a given day, flip to the back of a chapter, read an Attitude Kicker, and envision how you can infuse these principles into your life.

My mission is to renew your best attitude and re-kindle your enthusiasm and passion for life. My hope for you is that you enjoy your reading and, most of all, that it puts a positive kick into your life.

Sam Glenn

The Nation's Authority on Attitude™

A Kick in the Attitude Principle #1

Understand the Power of Your Kick

Years ago, a guy walked up to me in the freezing cold of winter and asked, "Do you have any jumper cables? My car battery is dead, I am super cold, and I want to get home."

Luckily, I had a set that I had received for Christmas – an odd gift, but you just never know. The cars I drove when I was down and out years ago taught me that jumper cables were a valuable asset. So I gave the guy's car a jump, and it started right up. With a smile and a new attitude to boot, he was happy to be out of the cold and on his way home.

What does this mean for you? I believe that we all have a deep desire to have our spirits lifted, inspired or motivated, or put another way, to have our lives "jumped." You may be thinking, I know someone who could use a good jolt right now – a family member, friend or co-worker. Or you might be the one who needs a good kick in the attitude, and that's okay to admit. There are certainly times when I do, and my friends and family are always happy to tell me as much.

A jolt to the attitude can change your way of thinking. If your thoughts and focus are not right or working in your favor, then you need to jolt your system a bit to get off that track of negative thinking and onto a track that profits your life.

What does this have to do with a kick?

The title of this book means just what it says; it's a kick in the attitude! But not in the sense that you may be thinking. Our "kick" is our best attitude working in a way that helps create an enriching life for us.

This "kick" in your attitude is everything that works for you. My goal is to rekindle the energy of this "kick" in your attitude, by helping you to recognize and choose the traits that feed it.

Each of the 13 attitude traits listed below will be highlighted in some way throughout this book. But as you will notice, they work, work, work for us, rewarding us in their own unique manner.

Here they are:

- **Courage**
- **Determination**
- **Perseverance**
- **Persistence**
- **Gratefulness**
- **Sense of Humor**
- **Patience**
- **Enthusiasm**
- **Faith**
- **Confidence**
- **Excellence**
- **Kindness**
- **Love**

Sometimes life has a way of knocking the kick out of us.

When we are excited about life, our attitude has such a kick to it that it's easier to tap more of our potential. When we feel better about ourselves, we perform better, are more creative, have more energy, treat others more kindly, and, as Nike says, have the passion to "Go for it." Whatever "it" might be!

But it isn't always easy to get the jumpstart we need. Years ago, when my life was encountering some pretty hefty challenges, I wanted to give up. I wallowed in self-pity and had no enthusiasm or passion. I was literally at a place where my attitude needed a swift kick.

Eventually though, I got the jolt that I needed and as a result, "I got my kick on!" I now have passion and enthusiasm, and I want to make each day count.

The fact of the matter is, it's easy to have a great attitude when life is good; but what about when life throws us a curve ball of adversity? Is your attitude ready for an attitude test? Because trials happen every day and they don't make appointments.

It's understandable that certain elements can knock the kick out of our attitude and life. We may get caught up, overloaded, uptight, and stressed out. Or life may simply become routine, causing us to level off and just go with the flow. As a result, we stop going for it, dreaming, creating and becoming. We skim by because we are tired and lack energy.

Maybe life has thrown you so many unexpected challenges that you are living in fear, filled with anxiety and doubt. Your attitude has taken a sharp turn south and you feel like you are walking in a cold shower.

We may not be able to control what happens to us or what goes on around us on a daily basis, but we do have the power to choose the attitude we bring to the situation, which can change the overall outcome. We can't change other people, but we can change ourselves, which can change the results. The key is not to leave our attitude to a role of the dice, but to put some purpose behind it and discover its true source of power.

To live a fulfilling and rewarding life, we need to know what is important to us. It's called knowing our priorities. I believe when we lose sight of our priorities, we lose ourselves.

Our attitude should always be a top priority because our attitude is the energy source and front line we use when we go at life, interact with others, and face obstacles. It's what functions through our skills, education and knowledge.

Is our attitude always going to be perfect? The answer is no; but it can always be better. And my simple philosophy is that life gets better when we get better. A great place to start in creating a better us, is to create a better attitude. And so now, without further adieu, it is time to get your Kick in the Attitude...!

Attitude Kicker

Imagine a black belt in karate, spinning, twirling, kicking so perfectly that his target is met "spot on" in an instant. Do you think he learned this kick overnight? Do you think he tried it once and had it mastered? Of course not. His kick took years to perfect, and he still makes mistakes.

So it is with getting your kick. You have that spark of life in you that can propel you to your target, but you have to practice, learn from those who have gone before you and are living around you, and be willing to start where you are.

Kick in the Attitude Principle #2

Get Over It and Get On With It

Life is about managing the things that we tolerate.

What are you no longer willing to tolerate?

What is currently bad enough for your life that you are willing to let it go?

Once while on an airplane flight with an overtired mind, I kept dwelling on a negative thought, watching it spiral and grow in my imagination. Eventually, I started turning red in my seat with anger. I would have kept on that path of thinking for another hour and my day would have been ruined had it not been for a big old cloud that shook our plane. When that plane hit turbulence, was I still thinking about my negative thought? Not at all. My pattern was broken, and my thinking interrupted. I had a new thought, wondering when the plane would stop jumping around! When the turbulence was over, I had a choice to make: I could either go back to thinking the bad thoughts that didn't benefit me in any way, or I could let the whole issue go and think about something that lifted my spirits. I had enough awareness of my thoughts that I could see the choice clearly, so I let my troubles go and built my day on a more productive outlook. All thanks to a nice jolt!

So whether you are dwelling on a little problem, or zapped by a jolt of turbulence, either way, the lesson is the same: get over it and get on with it! That's my philosophy when it comes to limitations that are getting in the way of achieving greatness or being our best. When I say get on with it, I am referring to moving to a place where you are not hung up, caught up or tripped up by your self-inflicted limitations, but are instead moving on and getting the best out of life and yourself. It takes courage and humility to take this step, but it is well within your power to do so.

So, let me ask you, is there something you are aware of that is keeping you hung up or distanced from where you want to be in life? Is there something blocking you from achieving your dreams and happiness? Is this thing keeping you from having fulfilling and connected relationships? What's in the way? Or maybe it is someone?

What is it for you? Is it...

1. Fear?
2. A past experience?
3. Laziness?
4. Someone who hurt you who you can't forgive or forget?
5. An excuse of some sort?
6. A negative attitude?

Whatever it is, you need to get over it and get on with it if you are ever to experience more of life. You can't get to the "more" until you overcome what's in the way of it. This is easier said than done, but the very act of making the decision to get over it means you are on your way. You have raised the bar for your life. You are ready to explore beyond your current boundaries, to see what life really has to offer you.

The process of overcoming limitations doesn't fully begin until you have a willingness to change, improve, and unlock the shackles you have placed upon yourself – willingly or unknowingly. To get the best out of life and yourself, you have to get real with yourself and address this question: what negative limitations are keeping you from your best – your best attitude, best choices, best thinking, best that life has to offer? Identify what is in the way – making you feel like you are in a rut, causing you to jostle up and down, preventing you from getting the promotion, making your relationships stale rather than enriched, keeping you from winning more sales, distracting those around you from cementing a common vision, igniting strife with co-workers, or distancing you from a healthy lifestyle. Ask yourself these questions:

Ask yourself these questions:

- **Do you complain a lot?**
- **Do you have a short temper– everything gets to you?**
- **Do you judge others and criticize?**
- **Do you believe nothing goes your way and that you are always a victim?**
- **Are you too controlling?**
- **Do you suffer from low self-esteem?**

It will be hard to accept anything else I am about to share in this book and actually see it work if you are hung up on something and not willing to face, conquer and move past it. Really, what's occurring is identity theft. Something is robbing you of your superstar status in life. And the purpose of knowing what's limiting you is that you will then know what you need to conquer.

Most limitations do not start on the outside of us; they start on the inside and work their way out. We create most of our own limitations. So, examine your limitations and work on overcoming them. When you do, the world around you will shift to seem better!

I recently received a letter from someone who had heard me speak on this point.

Dear Sam,

I have been trying to encourage a friend now for years. He was abused by his parents and has been seeing counselors with very little progress. He is always depressed. I am not sure what else I can do to encourage him. He is starting to bring me down. It's like he won't let go of the past.

My response:

It's always nice to know there are people like you who will reach out with a touch of encouragement. Sadly, your friend had an experience that is taking time to get through. Getting over it and on with it may happen in an instant or may take years. Our attitude plays a big role in that process. Your friend is not ready to let go of the past and as a result can't see what's in front of him. When our attitude is not right, nothing else appears right either. Your friend's limitation is not created by what happened to him, but by his tight hold on the experience, which is allowing it to rule his very existence. I might suggest putting some positive examples in front of him of people who have gone through similar situations, and have come out victorious. The best example I can give you is a woman who airs her talk show five blocks from my house. Her name is Oprah! Also, if your friend reaches out to help others who have battled or are battling the same situation, he will find renewed strength, because what we send out really does come back to us, and multiplied. He may even discover his calling and purpose. When bad things happen, we can choose to use them rather than let them use us. The only thing is, in order to turn it all around, we have to pinpoint what's limiting us and get over and get on with it. Your friend has to come to a crossroads and can decide it's time to get over and get on with it, that his life is worth much more than what he is currently believing or demonstrating. Be encouraging and don't give up. Remember, all encouragement makes a difference.

Sam Glenn

If you can't see the limitation, what do you do?

It may not be enough to hold a mirror to our lives, because we may not see anything wrong. Years ago, I wrote a letter to 26 people and proofed the letter 10 times. I thought I got all the spelling and grammar fixed, but to my surprise, my assistant pointed out that I had actually missed something. Something big. (And the letter had already been mailed. I had failed to have anyone else look it over before I sent it.) In the letter, I had indicated that I had matured over the years. But what it actually said was, "I have manured over the years." Two different experiences for the reader. I was so devastated because I thought, *How could I miss that? That of all things!*

The mistake was huge, but even though I reread my own letter 10 times, I didn't see it. The same occurs with our lives. If you have trouble finding the answers on your own, I suggest discussing the issue with someone you know who cares about you. He or she could be a friend, family member or counselor who may offer a unique and valuable perspective. Seeking the help of others is in no way an act of weakness, but instead demonstrates your active willingness to get over what's blocking you from getting the best out of life.

Ask this person if he or she sees a limitation in your life that you don't. Talk it out. Be prepared; you may not always hear what you want to hear. You may be told something that shocks you, or something you have heard over and over for years, but just ignored.

And I would add that it's good to ask what they see that is good about you and your life. Positive feedback is also very helpful. It has the force of encouragement and validates that not everything about you is negative. It gives you something to work from, to expand upon.

The key to making this work for you lies in your willingness to input constructive criticism in a positive way. It's not easy.

The first time I asked someone what limitations he saw in my life, I took his answer very personally. I wanted to bite him. I think I may have. I remember him saying a few words that I will never forget. Mind you, I was broke, in debt, and just trying to get by. I was living in a pity party and looking for sympathy, but my friend was not about to offer any. In fact, what he said really jolted my attitude. He said, "Sam, you don't have a hard knock life problem. What you have is an attitude problem. How do you expect to get ahead if you are always complaining and feeling sorry for yourself? You need to get your head out of your butt!"

When I let him out of the headlock I had him in and calmed down, I realized he had a point. (I didn't really put him in a headlock, but the thought was sure there.) He wasn't trying to knock me down or be distasteful to me. He really cared and believed that I was a person who was just sitting on a treasure chest of potential. But, as an adult, the last thing we want someone to tell us is that we have an attitude problem. It's a little humbling and the first thing we naturally do is get defensive. I felt like lashing back about what I thought was wrong in his life, but instead I took the road less traveled and used the information he gave me to my advantage. Life gets better when we get better, and that's how I applied the constructive input: to get better.

The question is, does the limitation standing in your way hurt enough for you to want to change? Consider this story... A young man was on a walk when he noticed a man rocking in a chair on his porch. Next to the man was an old hound dog. Every so often, the dog would yelp. The young man inquired, "Is that dog okay?"

"Sure, he is just lying on a nail," answered the old man.

"Well, why doesn't he move?" asked the young man.

"Guess it doesn't hurt him enough," the old man replied.

Your limitations, no matter how big, or how seemingly insignificant, will remain in front of you and affect your life in a negative way until you choose to change your mind and deal with them, get over them, and get on with it. Even those limitations that don't seem like a big deal are still affecting you. Why not get over them too?

Once you know what is getting in your way, it's up to you to summon the courage to *get over it and get on with it.* At some point, you have to be willing to let go of the limitation, and conquer it. You have to have a willingness to change: change your choices, your perspective, and your attitude.

Once you deal with your limitations, you will discover a spring in your step and a kick in your attitude. You will no longer need to yelp over those annoying nails. Instead, you can run around and bark!

Take a moment, flip to one of the blank pages at the end of this book and write down some limitations you believe you need to overcome. Then write down what think you need to do to overcome them. What has to change in your life? What do you think the result will be if you overcome your limitations? How will your life improve?

> **What would your life look like without your self-imposed limitations?**

Take ownership.

You are where you are, have what you have, and are getting what you are getting because of your choices. The world, your parents, your boss – nobody owes you a thing. You were born with your own set of wings. If you are not using your own wings, there is no one else to blame. You have to take responsibility for your life, because if you don't, who will? Don't blame everything and everyone for all your misfortunes. **We all face challenges that knock us down; the question is, what are you going to do about them?** Are you going to stay down and blame the world, or get up, grow up, and move on? When you stop blaming others and making excuses as to why you are living the life that you are, you will gain a new and refreshing perspective on life.

If we did all the things we are capable of doing, we would literally astound ourselves.

Thomas Edison

Unless you are mentally or extremely physically incapable, then you have NO EXCUSES – not a one. Even people with some unbelievable physical challenges overcome their obstacles to reach greatness. If you feel limited in your life, it is because you have allowed the negative thoughts, the past, or something else unsavory to be the master of your destiny. We are not perfect and we do not live in a perfect world. People will hurt us. Some will take advantage of us. We will make mistakes and fail, but BLAMING the government, the weather, or anything else does not get us to Candyland (our dreams).

Accepting responsibility for your future is one of the greatest steps you can take in drawing closer to your dreams. If something goes wrong or things get tough, accept it, live, learn and climb on. You can either sit on the side of the road and tell shoulda, woulda, coulda stories, or take ownership of your destiny and get moving.

When you are ready, let's move forward and continue working on that kick in your attitude. Now is the time!

Attitude Kicker

Think for a minute about Oprah Winfrey, who overcame her impoverished and abused childhood to go on to make millions and inspire the world. What if she had given up? Think of how many lives she has touched, and how blessed she is in return.

Why is it that some people get knocked down, and it propels them to success, and others get knocked down, and stay down? Sure, it helps to have people around us believing in us, but even if we don't, we can learn from those who pulled themselves up from their bootstraps, believing in their dreams when no one else did.

You have it in you to be what your dreams are made of. Get on with it!

A Kick in the Attitude Principle #3

Take Attitude Beyond the Mumbo Jumbo

The greatest discovery of my generation is that a human being can alter his life by altering his attitudes of mind.

William James

A fellow once walked up to me after one of my speeches and asked the question, "You don't really buy into that attitude mumbo jumbo do you?"

I smiled and said, "I sure do. When my attitude got better, my life got better." And then I posed a question for him, "What would your life look like or become if you did buy into all this attitude mumbo jumbo?"

Is attitude really more than just mumbo jumbo? You have to determine that for yourself, but what I have found is this: your attitude is the one string that plays a role in every single aspect of your life. It's either a force working for you or against you, and you determine which.

Close to 14 years ago, I bumped into a man by the name of Zig Ziglar, who by the way is one of the world's most profound Christian inspirational speakers. And when I say I bumped into him, I mean I literally almost laid him out flat! I didn't know who he was, but I had been given a free ticket to hear him speak. Before the event, I was trying to find a seat, and in my hurry and excitement, and without looking where I was going, I walked around a corner and ran smack into him. I apologized with great sincerity, cowered a bit, and waited for him to chew me out. But he had a great attitude about the situation. He just looked up at me and said, "Looks like you are in a rush there, big fella."

I said, "Yes sir. I have a free ticket to listen to a speaker by the name Zig Ziglar. I heard he is pretty good."

He looked up, gave me a vintage Zig Ziglar smile and said, "Well that's super good!" When I finally got to my seat, I was surprised to see that the very guy I just about knocked over was the guy now giving the speech. And one thing I will never forget: it was power-packed with wisdom on attitude.

I actually have had the chance to talk with Zig on three different occasions. One conversation was over the telephone while I was still in college. I wanted to interview him for our university paper, and he called me at 5:30am to talk about attitude. Here is the wisdom that I learned on developing a healthy attitude from Mr. Ziglar... He told me something like this, "If you do not like the output in your life (meaning your attitude), then you must change the input (what goes into your mind). What you feed the mind will govern your thinking, which will determine your attitude."

Mr. Ziglar also told me that he read an average of three hours a day. He said, "Sam, I realize what I put into my mind will come out through my words, actions and attitude." By choosing positive material, he was able to create what would become his life. This concept has stuck with me ever since, reminding me how important it is to feed my life with the type of material I want to exude.

So I ask you, what is flowing through you and creating your attitude? Think about what you are allowing to influence your attitude. What is feeding your words, actions, thinking, and beliefs? Input creates output. Take a brief moment and think about your environment and what you are allowing to influence you.

> **Attitude determines**
> **environment and performance.**
> **When we feel better, we do better,**
> **serve better, think better, and live better.**

Before I graduated from college, I applied for an internship with a very large firm that happened to be ranked number one in their industry. Everyone I knew wanted to work there. I remember thinking, if it is number one, it must be the best company to work for. It must be comprised of the most positive, upbeat people in the world.

I was wrong. There were so many negative, rude and depressing people there that I thought that whole number-one thing must be an oversight. It was quite shocking. There were times when I wondered how certain people around me even got hired. Some people were so rude and negative, I used to think, "I would hire that person, just so I could fire him!"

After being there a few weeks, I was becoming just like my environment. I was becoming rude, negative and depressed. I wanted to quit, but I stuck it out, thanks in part to an inspirational calendar my mom gave me as a gift. There were inspirational and motivational words on each day of the week. I would read them and repeat them to myself over and over all day long to get myself through the day.

Then I stumbled upon something so incredible, it changed my life. My mom gave me the calendar with the expectation that it would have a positive impact on my attitude, but when you are negative, you never think something like this can make a difference. But when it does – watch out! When something good soaks in and pushes the bad stuff out, your thinking changes, your responses change, your attitude changes and then your world changes.

That's what happened to me. Everything was changing and it was a good thing. I had been letting my emotions determine my behavior. Instead of letting that happen anymore, without even knowing it, my behavior – the words I read and repeated, and the way I moved my body – changed and influenced my emotions. I found a rhythm in my step, a smile on my face and a kick in my attitude. I took it a step further. I thought if those words can change me, perhaps they can change others around the workplace.

So, I took some initiative and attempted something somewhat risky, but something that could change the work environment. Right by my desk, there was a huge white board that was hardly used. So one day I took some colored markers and wrote inspirational quotes up there nice and big for all to see. The response was amazing. Everyone, and I do mean everyone, stopped to read them. The quotes would either put a smile on their faces, or a look that said, "Hmmm... Let me think more about that. That's good stuff."

I only had one person say to me, "You don't believe that junk do you?" I was like, "You need to go or get on board!"

One VP stopped by and was so inspired by the quote of the day that he would ensure that a new one would be up every day. He'd say, "I'll be back for the new quote tomorrow," to which I would reply, "I'll be looking for you!"

When I left that internship, they had a nice send-off party for me. And they all talked about how my attitude had touched their lives and made bad days better, getting them to think more clearly about life and what they were doing.

What I did was create an input of great material. And the result was that the overall actions and attitude of personnel improved. Can you do this? YES!

*Positive input can
change a negative environment.*

Action step: Read positive quotes every day. A positive quote per day will put a kick in your attitude. Post quotes where others can see them. I am not sure what your environment looks like (work or personal space), but whatever it is, it has a big influence on your attitude. The key for you is to be a thermostat and not a thermometer. The difference is, a thermometer adjusts to the temperature of the room while a thermostat determines the temperature of the room. To create an empowering environment, you have to create a positive flow of input.

Question: What things can you do to create a positive flow into your work environment? Are people critical, cynical and complicated in your environment? Then what small steps can you take or implement to change the environment to something more empowering and success enriching? Remember, most change like this is met with resistance, so take small steps and see what results you produce. I say if you have to work there, then make every effort to create an environment that fuels you, not pulls you down.

Attitude Kicker
What is attitude?

Attitude is the emotional response we have towards situations and people. It is the mental tone we emit. It is an outward expression of our thoughts and feelings. These thoughts and feelings can derive from many sources. They may come from our past experiences. They may be shaped by the stimuli we surround ourselves with: family, coworkers, or friends. They may come from what we listen to, what we watch on television, and what we read. Whatever feeds your mind and emotions feeds your attitude.

Take a moment and reflect on the current state of your attitude. What does it look like? If you put a face on it, would it be frowning or smiling? If it was a color, which one would it be? Has it been hurting you or helping you? Does it enhance your relationships at work and home, or erode them? If it were a magnet, what would it attract? Think of all of the things in your past that have been affected by or drawn into your life by your attitude. How is your attitude right now on a scale of 1 to 10 (1 being poor, and 10 being superstar)? If you are at a 6 or above, you are doing great. Anything below a 6, and you need to jumpstart your attitude – give it some life. I will present some very ideas on how to do that in a bit.

A Kick in the Attitude Principle #4

Don't Leave Your Attitude to Chance; Make It a Choice

Keep yourself clean and bright; you are the window through which you see the world.

George Bernard Shaw

I was once in the Newark Airport and was a bit stressed out looking for the rental car location. The airport was crowded and I got tense just being there. But off in the distance I heard something quite humorous and extraordinary: one guy singing. He was in charge of giving people information – where to go and how to get there. I walked over and asked how to get to the rental car place, and he sang me the directions. What an experience!

And not only did that guy make me feel good, he made the Newark Airport look good to me, and to all those other travelers.

I got to thinking about why I was so struck by this situation. The thing is, he worked in an environment where a lot of people would have been stressed out, burned out, or maybe even bored. But he chose to put on his best attitude and to conduct his work with excellence. In the process, not only did he have fun, but he changed the outlook and experience of those around him. What could have been a mundane or lifeless situation became unforgettable.

To choose to best nurture our attitude, it is important to first identify what can affect it in a negative way, so we can be prepared to defend ourselves from these stressors.

The four main elements that can make a good attitude vulnerable to becoming negative are:

1. Stress
2. Fatigue
3. Hunger
4. Negative Influences – family, friends, reading or listening materials, etc...

I am sure you have experienced all four at some time. Every day, we might encounter one of these four elements, or maybe all at the same time. And you may be the most positive person on the planet, but if your mind and body are encountering any of these elements, your attitude can be pulled to the dark side. Your dark-side outlook says, "Stay out of my way or endure my wrath!"

The value of recognizing these four elements is that in doing so, you become equipped with the awareness to identify them when they first confront you, and can thus do something about them before they make you negative. I think if we know what makes our attitude turn south, we are better able to combat and nip those things in the bud before they get bad. We can wash our window before it starts to impair our vision. It is easier to maintain a good attitude than it is to try to fix or overhaul a bad one.

The attitude you have boils down to a matter of choice. If you choose to maintain the right attitude, you must also choose to take the necessary steps to sustain your attitude.

Many years ago, I encountered all four elements at the same time; I was hungry, stressed, and tired, and people didn't seem to help the situation. I was invited to speak to 13,000 people on attitude, and I felt my attitude spiraling downward at sonic speeds. I had to catch a 6 am flight, and all they had for me was a middle seat, which at 6′7″, didn't thrill me. I had to run to my gate, and on the way, actually knocked over a family of 10; not really, it was just one guy, but everything felt amplified that day.

When I sat down on the airplane, it was obvious I didn't fit, and the woman next to me just laughed. As soon as we got in the air, the guy in front of me leaned his chair back. I thought to myself, "You've gotta be kidding." Then the guy next to me kept wanting to talk and had the worst breath in history. I had tears in my eyes. I would say I was in a good position to explode. My attitude went to the dark side. I was hungry, stressed, tired and ready to wrestle people to the ground.

I had to stop and remind myself, "Attitude is a choice. It's my attitude and it's my choice. What can I do to get back to my best attitude or at least a better attitude than I have now?"

When I got off the airplane, I got a bottle of water and a bag of pretzels and began talking to myself with empowering words. I probably looked like a nut, but I encountered some elements that can flip a great attitude over. As my pep talk progressed, I began to feel a little better and actually felt my best attitude coming back. But, my attitude was about to face a pop quiz. Read on...

It ain't over 'til you and 200 people see your underwear.

I was feeling back to normal again as I walked to pick up my luggage. I met my sponsor and we chit-chatted about the event. It was then that I heard an eruption of laugher. Curious what everyone was having such a good time about, I looked around to see somebody's luggage coming around the carousal with four pairs of underwear taped to the outside. At first, I started wailing in laughter. What better way to change my attitude than a little real-life comedy? I was ready to take advantage of the situation!

But then the contraption came closer, and the print on those Fruit of the Looms looked a little too familiar.

"WHAT THE...?!!!"

Apparently, the top of my luggage had ripped off and the baggage guys had reassembled it by putting the top part on first, my clothes on top of that, and then four pairs of underwear on top of that. I should mention that the tape covering it was the clear type.

I was beside myself trying to figure out what had happened. And to avoid escalating an embarrassing situation, I ignored my bag as it went around 13 times on the carousal. The hoot of it is, nobody left. They all wanted to see who owned the bag.

I faced a choice. I could react and get upset, but that really would not do anyone any good. So, I simply put a smile on my face and reached down to pick up the luggage. When I did, people laughed. One woman expressed to me that I made her day, all because I didn't get upset about it, but rather kept a good spirit.

How do you choose the best attitude? To create an attitude that works in our favor, we have to perform certain acts. Remember, emotion follows motion. Whatever you do that's good, your mood will follow. And the actions don't need to be hard. The key is not to complicate simplicity.

So don't complicate simplicity. Keep this process simple!

Here are a few ideas to help you get your best attitude to rise to the surface:

Feed your mind positive material.

I know we already mentioned that input creates output, but I can't stress it enough. What goes into the mind will come out in your words and actions. You must put good stuff in so good stuff comes out. There is a Bible passage in Romans 12:2 that says, "Do not conform any longer to the patterns of the world, but be transformed by the renewing of your mind."

A daily devotion is a super way to start your day and input good thoughts while the mind is fresh and waking up. Take 5 to 10 minutes and embrace something positive or inspirational. It can be an audio, video, or book. Quote books are a great source for feeding the mind. Listen to a motivational/inspirational audio CD, or good music that gets your blood pumping. When you eat breakfast, you are feeding your body and giving it energy to start the day. You must do the same for your mind. Feed it and give it energy. When you put healthy stuff into your mind, you are breathing life into your attitude.

What about the negative stuff that gets into our mind?

Experts tell us we should be drinking eight glasses of water a day. Why? Because it's fun to go the bathroom all day? No. It flushes our system of toxins. You drink that water to make your body healthy, to get rid of the junk that gets in there.

The same concept is true of our minds. Negative stuff gets in; that's a fact. It is up to you to wash it out. Renewing your mind involves clearing the garbage out. We have to detoxify our minds, or flush them daily. We do that by guarding what we let in. By wisely selecting who we hang around with, what we choose to believe, and what we listen to, watch and read, we are selectively deciding to fill ourselves with only the best. The more goodness you put into your mind, the more that it will wash out the negative. It's like taking a shower every day. Your body gets that attention; now summon the discipline to do the same for your mind.

Use uplifting, empowering words when you talk to yourself.

Change your self-talk. If you can, catch your inner dialogue in midstream and see what kinds of words you are using. If the tone is like, "Why try?" "I could never!" "What's the use?" or "I wish I could change this about my body," etc., then you need to change your language. Write down some positive statements that involve words like, "I can" or "I am" on a note card, and speak victory and empowerment into your life. Affirm your greatness and your potential.

*Nobody can make you
feel inferior without
your permission.*

Eleanor Roosevelt

Words are powerful, and you need to filter the words you hear around you as well. If you internalize the negative words people throw at you and play them over and over again until you start to believe them and own them, you block the door to your greatness. Instead, you have to release those words and replace them with truthful and empowering ones.

And it's okay to speak empowering words in advance. If today is a hard day, just say, "My day is hard now, but it's going to be awesome later."

Your self-talk is very powerful, and important to get you feeling your best, doing your best and going for your best. If you catch yourself beating yourself up with negative words, just take a moment to remind yourself of what you are doing, and get back to bettering your outlook with words that put a light to your path. And if people ask, "Why are you talking to yourself?" just tell them what I tell them, "I like to talk to smart, good-looking people!"

Look for the lighter side in situations.

Notice I did not say, "Look for the light at the end of the tunnel." Instead, make the most of your current situation, whatever it is. Plain and simple, some situations can be really stressful and perhaps tempt us to want to be negative or wallow in our darkness. But in every situation, there is a bright side or opportunity waiting to be discovered, right where we are. Take the time to think and look at the scenario from all perspectives.

Very importantly, ask someone or several trusted people to help you see what you are not seeing. Others can provide glimpses into a huge source of brightness. There are times when I have struggled with seeing the lighter side, and when I get the input of someone else, it opens my eyes to be more understanding and to deal with things in a more effective and healthy way.

Sing like a rock star!

I know this one sounds off the wall, but it works. Sing. Play some music loudly and sing to it. I like singing to The Temptations,' "I've got sunshine on a cloudy day." Even if you sound bad, that's okay. Sing. It will improve the quality of your mood (and maybe your voice). And move to it too, while you are at it. Just try it.

Exercise, eat right and rest up.

Your health has a huge impact on your attitude. When you work out on a consistent basis, your body releases endorphins, which relieve stress and actually improve the quality of your mood. Get your body moving. Go for a walk. Get a trainer. Do something four days a week for a minimum of 30 minutes. As you burn calories, you are also burning stress, which clears your mind, improves your mood, and opens the door for you to touch your potential.

Eat healthy.

The way we eat and what we eat has a direct impact on our mind and body. Food should be used to create energy, not to stuff ourselves to the brink. Use food correctly, and it will impact your attitude in a positive way. I recommend eating small portions, not big heavy ones that will make you tired (like I and I think a lot of others tend to do on Thanksgiving). Eat that which will give your mind and body energy and life: fruits, vegetables, meats, nuts, beans, and rice. Don't eat late at night either. If you eat too late, your body will be working all night trying to digest food, when it should be resting and reviving you with energy.

Smile.

Smiling makes you look good, feel good and attract

others. Practice smiling more often.

Beware of toxic attitudes (people).

Some people have poor and negative attitudes and don't even realize it. Other people can find the joy in any situation. There is a story of a man sitting next to a woman in church. The woman yells out, "Whew! It sure smells like someone's deodorant is not working!" The fellow next to her says, "Well it sure can't be mine; I am not wearing any!"

Funny, but true. Some people just don't recognize how sour their attitude is or has become. But we all have the opportunity to turn the situation around, to create something fruitful out of something negative.

Be on guard for the attitudes that defeat you. Misery loves company and it's always recruiting. Negative people have one goal in mind, to pull you down. Remember, it's not the water around the boat that causes it to sink; it's the water that gets into the boat.

These negative attitudes will keep you from your best. They are what turn a healthy attitude into a toxic attitude.

Guard yourself from negative people by:

- Guarding your time with them.
- Guarding your mind from their negative words.

Get real!

It's time to step into your own personal evaluation chamber and do an assessment of your attitude. Ask those close to you what kind of attitude they think you have. Now be ready; it might not be the words you want to hear. If they say you are negative, or up and down, or dry, it's an opportunity for you! It's an opportunity for you to improve, make it right, and get healthy.

I said that attitude is the heart of success. In health terms, the number one killer of human beings is heart disease. In terms of life success, the number one killer is attitude. If it's not healthy, don't get mad or flip out. Fix it. Make some new choices and be open to changing. Begin a daily exercise program focused on building a superstar attitude.

Don't fear this time, but seize it. You are jolting your attitude, charging it up and giving it life. Could you imagine if you didn't change the oil in your car... ever?! That car would not operate at its best. It needs attention every 3,000 miles. The human mind is the same way. It needs daily attention to operate at its best for you.

Attitude Kicker

Skills are a necessity for success. But when you mix your skills (education, experience, abilities) with the right attitude, you become a superstar. Your attitude is what functions through your skills, education, experience, and abilities, determining if you are an average maker or a difference maker. If your skill level is the same as 100 other people, the one string that will separate you from the crowd is the right attitude.

It is also important to remember that a lack of skills cannot be made up for by a great attitude, no matter how positive you may be. I have a great attitude, but you don't want me to fly your plane or perform heart surgery on your loved ones. You get the point. Get the right skills you need to succeed, but most importantly, mix it with the right attitude and your results will be greatness!

A Kick in the Attitude
Principle #5

Discover Your Music (Purpose) and Live It Out Loud!

If you want to get somewhere, you have to know where you want to go and how to get there. Then never, never give up.

Norman Vincent Peale

Here is a story of two guys who discovered that dreams and purpose can come true, but not without persistence and perseverance. In 1989, Bert and John Jacobs designed their first tee shirt. For five years, the brothers hawked tee shirts on the streets of Boston and traveled the East Coast, selling door to door in college dormitories. Their efforts were not very prosperous. They lived on peanut butter and jelly, slept in their van, and showered when they could.

By the fall of 1994, heading home from a long, less-than-fruitful road trip, Bert and John were desperately searching for answers to keep the dream alive. One fateful September day, they printed 48 shirts with a character they created who had a very funny grin – Jake. The tee shirts also said the words "Life is Good."

By noon, all 48 of those tees were gone. Soon, Jake and the Life is Good message were introduced to local retailers, and the simple message of optimism was embraced like nothing the brothers had ever seen. They discovered their purpose by leaving no stone unturned. As a result, they now do more than just run a business; they give back to the community and donate their time and resources to make a difference. How's that for discovering your purpose?!

You just never know when, where or how your life's purpose will be discovered. Purpose comes from knowing what you want out of life. You find your ultimate purpose in life when you find something you really care about. Purpose involves living for a cause; having a mission; or fostering a burning desire in the heart to do something, have something, go somewhere, be something, give something or build something. There is no limit when it comes to what your true purpose in life could be. You may even discover your purpose in the most unexpected ways. It may come at the end of a series of disappointments, but you just never know when, where or how purpose will be birthed into our life. The following story is a perfect example of that.

We are all born with a purpose. It's there! You may have to uncover a few stones to discover it, but it exists. And once you find it, life as you know it will never be the same.

Define what you desire.

If you don't know where you are going, any road will get you there.

Lewis Carroll

Could you imagine if I asked you to go hunting with me and we just stood outside the woods and randomly shot into the forest? We'd have no clear vision of what we were hunting.

Getting a reward starts when we define what we want. We need a target to hit or we will waste precious time and energy aiming at nothing and therefore hitting nothing.

We need a vision for our lives. We can't just expect we will achieve success by randomly buying every infomercial product stating we will become rich by working three to five hours per week. Success just doesn't work that way.

Plus, you want a vision that gets your blood moving, something you have feelings about. It's got to be something worthwhile to move towards, giving you hope and enthusiasm. We need a dream that inspires and motivates us to live with purpose and passion. If you set your mind and heart to something, there is no telling what you will achieve.

Purpose-filled people believe in the incredible, see the invisible, look for the good, hear the great, and shoot for the stars

It is not enough just to define our goals. We have to give goals life by writing them down on paper, thinking about them, acting on them and eventually feasting on them! The law of attraction will help if you do the right things. Take time to clarify what it is you want out of life and then make a plan stating what it will take to get there.

If you have no clue what you want, where do you start? Start with something small if you need to prove to yourself that it really does work, or if you need to practice finding things to strive for. Then get crazy when it comes to setting goals for your life!!! Why? Because number one, you are worth it, and if you are not getting what you want out of life, do you really think you are going to be happy and fulfilled? Probably not! So set some goals that will give your life more depth, meaning and value. Get yourself a goal journal and begin writing in it – what you want, how you plan to achieve it, why you want it, what it looks like, down to the color and smell. Whatever you want to write that will make your vision more real… Write it out.

Then go back and visit your writing periodically, adapting it to make it better as you go and learn more about what life has in store for you. But don't give up!

Persistence plus purpose creates greatness.

Persistence is holding on to something positive and not ever letting go despite the circumstances.

I once saw a little girl in the grocery story wrapped around her mother's leg screaming, "I won't let go! I won't let go of you, Mama!"

What a perfect example of persistence. Why do we need to mix persistence with our purpose? Things get in the way – distractions, setbacks, roadblocks – all of which try and throw you off your path. The key is not giving up. If one plan doesn't work, try it a different way.

Giving up is easy. Imagine driving in a car with a friend and you hit a dead end. Your friend stops, turns off the car, looks at you and says, "I guess it's over."

"What's over?" you ask.

"Life. It's a dead end. We can't go any further," replies your friend.

You would be like, "Turn this car around and let's

find a way!"

It seems silly, but so many of us have this conditioned mental pattern that when it seems like we've hit a dead end, we just give up. Could you imagine if the doctor was operating on a loved one and the surgery got a little challenging, and the doctor just gave up? Giving up does not feed our purpose, but persistence does.

Ever heard of Colonel Sanders, the founder of Kentucky Fried Chicken? When he got his first Social Security check, he realized that it would not be enough to live off of. So he thought about what he could do to make money. His idea was to offer his chicken recipe to restaurants. He only asked to split the profits of all the chicken that was sold. He set out with his proposal, and in a very short time was rejected close to 1,000 times before he got a yes. All I can say is, he must have really believed in that chicken recipe, 'cause he didn't give up! He applied persistence and it paid.

It's challenging when the odds are set against you, but persistence and perseverance never let us down. We can achieve our dreams, and make our ideas a reality if we pursue them with enough vigor.

Having a proactive attitude does not take away the setbacks we will encounter in life... But the right attitude will empower us to deal with setbacks more quickly and in a more profitable way.

Are there going to be moments when you fail, or get rejected and criticized in your pursuit of achieving your dreams and goals? Sure, that's all a part of pursing anything worthwhile. Hear me again, it's a part of the process. Setbacks don't mean "quit." The key is to make sure that your belief and passion outweigh the setbacks. If they do, then you can make it. A setback should be a clue that you are getting closer to achieving your goal. Thomas Edison was once asked what he thought about failing more than 2,000 times in his pursuit of inventing the light bulb. His response was, "I didn't fail 2,000 times, I just discovered 2,000 ways not to invent the light bulb." But what he also found out is that each failure got him closer to the goal. He didn't set a limit on achievement. He didn't say, "Look team, if we don't find a way to invent a light bulb after 50 attempts, let's just call it quits and build a giant candle." He was determined to get through the failed attempts, rejections and criticism.

*Success is going from one
failure to another without
losing enthusiasm!*

Sir Winston Churchill

If you drive down any busy street in almost any town, chances are you will see a Wendy's restaurant. A guy by the name of Dave Thomas, who dropped out of the 10th grade, started from scratch and made his dream a reality. Did he encounter adversity and failure? You betcha! But it did not determine his outcome. What about Wal-Mart? If you read Sam Walton's book, *Made In America*, you will learn about all the challenges he faced getting Wal-Mart off the ground. It wasn't easy, but the setbacks and obstacles did not keep him from giving up.

What about Jim Carrey? He is a guy who at one time was living with his family in a van and tents on the front lawns of relatives, because they had no home or money. Jim didn't let his humble background limit his ability to achieve his dreams. It didn't happen overnight, but it did happen through perseverance.

What each of these people demonstrated was an ability to use failures as stepping stones. If you personalize your failures in a big way, then you give those failures a big life. But if you treat your failures as part of the process necessary to achievement, then you give only a small life to them. A failure with a little life doesn't have as much control over your choices, future actions, and emotions.

Take the time to appreciate and learn from those who have gone before us to encounter and overcome failure, achieving their desired successes. Some are well known, and yet some might just be local business people in your town. Value the wisdom that failure taught them. It may help you avoid pitfalls and possible failures in your life. Success leaves clues. Decipher and use them.

Attitude Kicker

*Stop waiting and procrastinating
and just start!*

A young lady approached me after one of my presentations and enthusiastically expressed her deep passion and desire to sing. She said, "I love to sing! I believe it's my gift!" She was really enthusiastic, but had no idea where to begin in making her dream become real. I looked at this young lady and gave her the same advice that was given to me. I told her, "Go outside, pick up a rock, toss it up and wherever it lands, start there."

Well, call me crazy, but that really is what you have to do if you have a goal, a vision or something you desire to go after. Just start where you are. Where else are you going to start? You can't start any place other than where you are at this moment. Start simple and start small. Ask questions, practice, learn, research, knock on doors, make phone calls, read, get involved, attend seminars, listen to tapes— do whatever it takes to get the ball rolling on your dream. If you are going to build anything worthwhile in your life, you have to start somewhere. Starting means taking action now. Start now, this minute. Start where you are. Start broke if you have to, but START!

A Kick in the Attitude Principle #6

Seize the Opportunities in Your Adversities

The only people without problems are in a cemetery.

Norman V. Peale

During the late 1960s, a couple was vacationing in the California mountains, where a pleasant-looking young man was sitting by a bridge near their hotel. Day after day, they saw him sitting in the same spot. Finally, on the last day of their vacation, the elderly couple had to ask the man, "Why do you sit in that one spot all day, every day?"

He replied, "I happen to believe in reincarnation. I believe that I have lived many times before and will have many more chances to live a different life. This life hasn't been that good for me, so I am sitting this one out and waiting for the next life to come along."

Life is good when it's good, but what about when life throws us curve balls? We are required to respond. And by no means is it easy. When life presents us with an unscheduled appointment with adversity, we have to adopt the mindset that there are opportunities within that adversity. That's perseverance in action. It's easy to throw in the towel, but it doesn't make life better. Adversity can easily give birth to fear, doubt and discouragement, but through an attitude of perseverance, we can summon the courage to push on, bounce back and not give up.

Years ago, I worked for a guy that would answer any challenge with the thought, "What a great opportunity." I thought the guy was nuts or had been dropped a lot as a kid. But in reality, he had the right

attitude. His attitude allowed him to perceive opportunity amidst the adversity. My attitude at the time
could not allow me to see my problems that way, al-
though through the years, I have gained that skill.

Adversity is an unscheduled appointment
that will test your resilience.
But, with the right attitude, you will be able
to overcome the situation and gain valuable
wisdom for future unscheduled appointments.

Eleven years ago, I found myself in a whirlwind
of adversity. I was flat broke, in debt, and sleeping
on borrowed floor space in my mom's one-bedroom
apartment. My only source of income was from delivering newspapers at 2am three nights a week, until I
eventually started work as a nighttime janitor.

My ambition reached an all-time low. I had graduated from college on a full-ride basketball scholarship,
acquired my first and second job within a year, and
been fired from both. At the time, I felt as if I had no
purpose in my life. There was nothing to get excited
about. I had only enough enthusiasm to get by. The
fear of trying again sat heavily in my gut. What if I
failed again?

On the side, I had been running a company my
grandfather had operated for 30 years before entrust-

ing it to our family before his death. I had no clue how to manage the business. My act of throwing out conventional wisdom, spending money unwisely, and not investing proper care or attention would result in huge consequences.

Just when I thought things could not get worse, I received a phone call from the people who stored and packaged my products. The woman on the other end of the line told me there had been a fire and everything was lost.

Just like that, it was over. In its place was a huge financial hole which forced me to declare bankruptcy. At the courthouse, I glanced around at the others in my shoes, wondering how they had gotten there, feeling like I didn't belong. Then, it was my turn to verbally verify my debts into a tape recorder. Hearing my own voice listing my failures in front of public witnesses drove it home. I had failed.

Shortly thereafter, I was invited to have coffee with a concerned friend, complaining and venting all the while. Misery loves company, and I was recruiting. I felt unlucky. I didn't care about anything. He smiled, pulled out a piece of paper, and made me list what I had to be thankful for. At first, I could not think of a thing, but as he made suggestions, the list began to grow. I had food to eat, a place to sleep, people who loved me, shoes to wear, a toothbrush to use.

> *The fastest way to put your attitude back into perspective is to look at what you have to be grateful for in your life.*

I began to see a twilight of hope. Instead of focusing on what was negative in my life, I began to see what was good.

We then continued to discuss my interests. I was teaching Sunday School, which seemed to be the one activity I enjoyed. Somehow offering encouragement to others made me feel invigorated. So we created a simple plan to build a speaking career and impact others, laying out the actions I needed to take.

I slowly and painfully began building my new life. I came home from working nights, slept a few hours, got up and called hundreds of people, letting them know I was an inspirational speaker with a great message. Something in me was driven to find a way forward, whatever it took, despite having almost no experience or proof that it would ever work. I was equipped with a proactive attitude and ready to discover new horizons.

For a year, the only result I got was a large phone bill. Nobody called me back. Those around me told me to give up, and pursue a "real job."

Eventually, I gave in. I dusted off my resume and

faxed it to a few companies, garnering an immediate call from a mortgage firm in downtown Chicago. At the interview, I was hired on the spot.

It took me an hour and a half to commute to work and almost two hours to get home. At lunch on my first day, I sat in a Burger King, realizing I had just sold out on my dream.

That night, I paced and wrestled with what to do. It was 2am and I had to be up in three hours. I prayed. And it hit me that if I went to that job tomorrow, I would be leaving my dream further behind. Maybe nobody had yet called me to speak, but if I continued with this job, I would be turning my back on something I knew I was called to achieve.

I got on the phone and very quietly, with my mom awkwardly in the next room, left a voicemail for my new boss: "Sir, I want to thank you for hiring me. But I can't work for you at this time. I have a dream that I was called to do. I hope you understand."

The next day, I shared my decision with my mom. I don't think she fully supported it, but I simply asked her for one thing: just believe in me.

Two weeks passed from the time I quit my job. The phone finally rang. The first message went something like this: "We got your materials and were wondering if you would like to come speak to about 20 teachers. If they like you, they may invite you to their schools to speak to their students."

I was thrilled. I had my first, official, non-paying speaking engagement.

On the day of the event, I loaded my '82 Buick Regal for the two-hour drive. It was a car that took a lot of faith to own, as it always seemed to be running on a prayer.

As I arrived, the gas light went on. I had forgotten my wallet, not that it would have helped, since I had nothing in it. Panic struck. My speech was about to go from, "Teachers, you've got to believe in yourself," to, "Excuse me, Sir, can I borrow a dollar?"

I didn't want to let my situation show, so I set up my stuff and gave what was in my mind the absolute worst speech ever.

Not only did I speak, but I visually demonstrated my message through an oversized chalk-art drawing set to music, carefully designed to be very captivating. On this day though, my picture was barely recognizable.

Most people got up, waved from the back, and walked out of the room. I got an old familiar feeling again. I had worked so hard to get here and failure was showing its face.

I thought, "You should just quit. You worked an entire year on this dream and this is what you do! You are going to live with your mom forever."

As I was packing up, a fellow reached over and touched me on the back. "Excuse me, Sam, can I talk with you? I want to thank you for your presentation today. Could I have that picture you drew? It's so beautiful."

I was thinking, he has eyesight problems!

"Sam, I need to let you know, I didn't want to come today. I lay in bed for an hour staring at the walls. I have been depressed. I recently got a divorce and never get to see my kids. But today, I got something powerful from your message. You talked about believing in yourself, but I didn't get that. I got hope, love and encouragement. And I want to thank you. This picture is going to go on my wall at home. Sam, don't stop doing what you're doing; you are going to touch a lot of people's lives."

My dream was speaking to me: "Don't give up! Not yet!!" What I saw as junk, someone else saw as beauty.

He walked away with tears in his eyes. I had made a difference to one person. I thought, I can do this!

I was overwhelmed by the glee of the moment, until I got to my car and the reality of not having any gas or money set in. I sat there thinking, praying. Moments later, I heard my name, "Sam! Wait!" It was that guy again. Little did he know, I wasn't going anywhere!

He came over, thanked me again, and then did something odd. He took his hand, put it into my pants pocket, and walked away smiling. I slowly reached down and pulled out a $100 bill. I was in complete shock. It was a miracle, my harvest coming in. I had sowed the seed, planted the dream, not really knowing where or how I would be rewarded. And today was the day.

I never looked back. I spent the next 10 years perfecting my craft, speaking to groups and motivating others for change. Today, I have reached more than 2-million people, and even spoken alongside celebrities, all because of the encouragement of a few people, including that man, who may never know the impact he had on my life.

So the next time you get rejected, criticized, challenged and collide with failure, get excited. It's a sign: You've entered the land that lies just at the border of your dream.

Life is 10% what happens to me and 90% how I respond.

Chuck Swindall

What adversity has taught me about life.

1. There is a gift in failure.

Or said a different way, there are opportunities in our adversities. The gift of failure is that sometimes our life purpose can come from our ashes. When something doesn't work out, we have to be willing to rebuild, get up and try again. Getting thrown off the horse isn't fun, but sometimes it means that a better horse is out there waiting for us.

2. Act with courage.

When life sends us an unscheduled appointment with adversity, it's easy to get scared and react with fear, discouragement and doubt. I remember a creditor calling about a bill that I had no money to pay, and I was so scared I sold my truck the next day, but the result was I had no way to get home or to work. I was worse off because my fear got the better of me. Acting with courage empowers us to gain the confidence to know that we can conquer our challenges. The wisdom you will gain in facing your fears will be invaluable to future encounters with adversity.

3. Be grateful.

It's easy to feel sorry for yourself when things are going badly. But the fastest way back to a perspective of clear thinking is through looking at what you have to be thankful for in your life. Take out a piece of paper and write down everything you can be thankful for right now. It might be that you have a toothbrush. It can be anything – shoes, a pillow, a friend, a blue sky outside. Put that paper in your pocket or post it up, and refer to it often, whenever you feel yourself drifting into a self-pity party.

4. This too shall pass.

Your present situation is not permanent. Life keeps moving. If we think life will never get better, then our thoughts become unhealthy. The words and actions that follow often create a defeated mentality, limiting our potential and achieving power. I believe there is a season to mourn, grieve, and acknowledge our pain or situation, but when the season is over, it's over. Move on. It's time for a new season of rebirth, with new choices, new thinking – the works.

5. Create a new perception for your life.

Affirmations of a new perception for you can be…

I am no longer a victim, but a victor.

I am more than able to overcome this situation.

I am bigger than my failures!

I was born with the ability to achieve and live my dreams.

I have options and solutions.

I am going to get up and make something happen today!

Attitude Kicker

Persistence can turn your idea, vision or dream into a reality.

Everything around you started with an idea in someone's mind, which he or she acted on. The road to making these dreams a success was not paved with simplicity and ease. It was challenging, frustrating, scary, and discouraging, and I assure that there were moments when the dreamers questioned themselves, their purposes, and/or dreams. Perhaps thoughts of giving up crossed their minds, and maybe they even began to believe the negative words of their critics, but the principle of persistence and perseverance kept them going. A burning passion within them kept them up late at night, searching for a way, trying to find answers that would work. That same passion got them up early in the morning, sacrificing laziness for dedicated effort. It got them searching for the right people to help. It got them knocking on doors for people to believe in them, their dreams and ideas. They learned from their failures, battled the emotions of defeat, and as a result, ended up in the winner's circle.

A Kick in the Attitude Principle #7

Believe in Your Greatness!

When you doubt yourself, you defeat yourself.

When you believe in yourself, you win.

As I sat there humped over my dinner, I could not stop the tears from rolling down my face. I had my heart set on a basketball scholarship. But it seemed like a faint wish at this point that would not come true. I had injured my knee a few months before and the recovery was going slowly. I had just returned home from a basketball practice wherein my coach told me how disappointed he was in me and my performance. I had very little confidence in myself and I could understand my coach's frustration. I was a team leader and my injury was hurting the team. I was not performing up to my previous ability. I sat there at a crossroads and contemplated quitting. I knew quitting would not show leadership but I didn't want just to sit on the bench.

As I sat there trying to eat what my mom had kept warm for hours, I opened up the newspaper. Every other Thursday the area newspaper would show the statistics of all the top area players – points averaged per game, rebounds, and all that good stuff. After the start of the season, I was at the bottom in almost every category and non-existent on the rebound list. It was embarrassing. I was a big man averaging less than six rebounds a game. According to my position and stature, it was my role on the team to get rebounds, but I was not living up to that expectation.

I was dead last in the rankings, and instead of wallowing one more minute in my situation, I made up my mind right there that I was going to turn it all around. My goal was to go to the top. It was an outrageous goal, because I was in the company of some incredible players. I knew it would be a tough race and a long shot, but I was at the bottom with only one place to go: up. I had nothing to lose by aiming and shooting for the top. So I set my heart and my mind to it and away I went...

For weeks, rebounding was all I could think about. I would see my name being listed as number one on the statistic sheet for area rebounds. I would visualize myself going after every rebound.

My performance turned around dramatically. My body was following the path in which my mind believed. My teammates and coach could not believe the turnaround.

I still had some odds set against me. I was rehabilitating an injured knee. I wore an Omni brace, which is a huge leg brace that keeps your knee stable, preventing a blow-out. While it protected my knee, it added weight and took time to get used to.

When game time came, I was a maniac. I was almost crazy out there. It wasn't long before I found myself moving toward that picture in my mind. I was getting 10 rebounds a game, then 15, then 18, and then 22. If that ball came off the rim, I knew it was mine! My hands became glue. In fact, one of my teammates picked up on what I was doing and he started going after rebounds like nuts. He went from averaging 4.5 rebounds to getting 9, 12, and sometimes 15 rebounds a game. My drive and determination raised the level of my teammates' play as well. As I write this, I have goose bumps because it was so incredible!

Weeks passed into the season and I wasn't sure where I stood in the ratings. I saw my name on the bottom of the list, and in the middle, but didn't stop believing in reaching the top. The final Thursday in which I would see the year-end standings came. I was nervous on the car ride home from practice. I want to point out that I didn't tell anyone what I was doing and believing in, not even my family. My goal was strictly personal. As I walked in the front door, I could see the paper sitting on the counter next to my dinner. I felt like Charlie in Willy Wonka and the Chocolate Factory, when he opened up the chocolate bar to win the golden ticket. I ate a few bites of my dinner and slowly opened the paper to the standings page. I glanced really quickly and didn't even see my name on the list. My heart skipped a beat and I thought, this can't be right. I have been averaging so many rebounds. I took a deep breath and looked again, and then I realized why I didn't see my name at first. I was looking at the bottom of the list, to make sure I wasn't there, and the middle, because that's where I had been most recently. But, when I looked at the very top to see who was the number one rebounder, it read these words: SAM GLENN.

I put the paper down on the counter and started to cry because I had reached my goal. It took so much hard work and determination, but in that moment I tasted what true victory in reaching your goals is all about. I honestly wasn't sure if I could do it or not, **but I tried and gave it my very best**. I set my heart and mind to it, envisioning and acting upon it, and it happened – even more perfectly than I would have imagined.

> *Building confidence in yourself is a daily process. Step by step, you can rebuild, or build from scratch on the confidence you have.*

The change in my attitude was my decision to define what I wanted, and then start believing in myself and my ability to achieve my objective. It is true – you really can achieve greatness when your heart and mind are fully in it. Tapping your potential starts with believing in yourself. When you doubt yourself, you defeat yourself. When you believe in yourself, you have everything to gain and nothing to lose. Believing in yourself should not be an ego thing, but rather a confidence thing. It means knowing you have what it takes to achieve, move forward and attract what you desire into your life. If you battle feeling insecure, or have failed in the past and are experiencing a sense of fear, you need to refer back to the principle, "Get Over It and Get On with It."

It's okay to believe in yourself. It's good to believe in yourself. And yes, some people may say some cruel things to you and try to keep you down, but you don't have to listen to them. You get to choose what to accept.

Think of it this way... If you had an authentic and rare diamond with astronomical value, what would you think if a group of people came up to you and spouted, "That's not real! It's worth only about $10.00. It's nothing!"

You would know that what they were saying was false, because you would know the truth!

When you realize who you are, and the greatness and potential you possess, the same truth will apply. Someone will almost always put you down and try to keep you from the prize, but knowing the truth frees you from the lies and even prevents you from considering the negative comments of others.

Give yourself permission to believe in the greatness of who you are, and when you do, incredible things will happen in your life.

Here is a truth to embrace and live by:
You are a person of worth and value and
nobody can take that away from you.
Once you believe that and embrace it in your
mind and body, your confidence will build and
the results can be seen.

Attitude Kicker

*Attitude empowers us to
fight the good fight.*

Consider an even more compelling angle from which to see how crucial a role your attitude plays in your life... When a person has cancer, he or she usually begins treatment to combat the disease. But medical experts understand that radiation and medication can only do so much fighting. The rest is left up to the individual's attitude. Major universities have been studying the effects of mindset and attitude on health, publishing convincing results. But, you might argue, what about those who don't survive, yet had a positive attitude? A healthy attitude will serve you better than a negative attitude will in anything and everything. You do the math.

A Kick in the Attitude
Principle #8

Life is Short, So...
Lighten Up!

The human race has only one really effective weapon, and that's laughter.

The moment it arises, all our hardnesses yield, all our irritations and resentments slip away, and the sunny spirit takes their place.

Mark Twain

A man appeared before St. Peter at the pearly gates. "Have you ever done anything of particular merit?" St. Peter asked.

"Well, I can think of one thing," the man offered. "On a trip to the Black Hills, out in South Dakota, I came upon a gang of macho bikers who were threatening a young woman. I directed them to leave her alone, but they wouldn't listen. So I approached the largest and most heavily tattooed biker. I smacked him on the head, kicked his bike over, ripped out his nose ring and threw it on the ground, and told him, 'Leave her alone now or you'll answer to me.'"

St. Peter was impressed, and asked "When did this happen?"

"Just a couple minutes ago," replied the man.

This was just a taste of humor to get this chapter rolling. In fact, this just might be my favorite chapter. I love humor. If there is one attitude trait that makes life worth living, it's having a sense of humor. Let me ask you, do you know anyone who is really uptight? Do you see it as a quality that enriches that person's life or hurts it?

The answer is obvious. I think a lot of people, honestly, are just way too wound up and miss the value of humor and its benefits. The bottom line is we need to lighten up!

What does it mean to lighten up? It means choosing to look at the lighter side of a situation. It's a healthy perspective in which we view the humor around us, enjoying and even celebrating it with others. Humor is like a muscle; in order for it to be effective, it has to be worked. Let's explore a few ideas on how to fortify your humor muscle.

Humor has power-packed benefits.

Humor has the health-promoting power to create wellness in your life. When you laugh or have a lightened-up mood, the human body releases endorphins into your system. Endorphins are a group of chemicals that reduce pain, contribute to healthy sleep, improve the quality of moods, and heal the body.

The opposite happens when you let tension build up. When your body suppresses negative emotions, you are at a higher risk for illness, anxiety, depression, mood swings, anger and frustration. When you allow yourself to live in a state that has limited "humor activity," you can actually age more quickly and become less attractive. We don't even need validation for why we wouldn't want that. Envision someone who is really uptight versus someone who is laughing, enjoying good humor, and smiling; who might you say appears to have more appeal? Hands down, the person who is using their humor attitude wins.

Another benefit to having a good sense of humor is that it will give you the coping power to deal with whatever life throws your way. It does not mean that you will avoid all negative emotions. It means that your body and mind will help you respond more favorably in order to combat your thoughts and moods with emotions such as hope, joy, love, optimism and caring.

According to Dr. Bill Fry at Stanford University, laughing 200 times burns off the same amount of calories as 10 minutes on a rowing machine. Laughter oxygenates your blood, increases energy, and relaxes your muscles. Studies are showing that laughter also strengthens your immune system.

Many hospitals today are incorporating what is known as "laugh therapy" or "humor programs." The purpose is to help in a speedy recovery. Do you remember the movie *Patch Adams*, and how he used humor to lift people's spirits? Patch felt that it was a necessary part of healing. Today, hospital beds are filled with people who have stress-related illnesses, meaning they could get up and go **physically**, but **mentally they need inspiration.**

In 1964, Norman Cousins brought to the attention of the medical community that laughter heals the body and lifts the spirit. He had a debilitating disease called ankylosing spondylitis. His physicians gave him little hope for recovery. Norman read a book by Hans Selye about how the body responds to stress. It illustrated how negative emotions could create chemical changes that would lead to exhaustion. He suspected that the positive emotions such as faith, hope, and joy might create changes within the body that might enhance the recovery process. Since the behavior of laughter opens the door to these positive emotions, Cousins began to watch funny movies to stimulate laughter. He noticed that after each episode, he would sleep better and need less medication. His body began to heal. I especially love the story about how he took his apple juice and poured it into the cup they used to take urine samples. The nurse walked in and saw the cup and the color and said, "Norman, this does not look right." Norman grabbed the cup from her and said, "You are right, I guess I better run it through again." And he drank it. The nurse just about passed out! Norman just laughed!

You are your best source for humor.

If we simply choose to lighten up and look around and at ourselves, we will discover an abundance of humor. The sign of a healthy attitude is when we can laugh at ourselves. Someone once said, "The ability to laugh is God's gift to us. To act on that ability is our gift to ourselves. To share that laughter is our gift to others."

Over the years, I have had to learn to see the humor around and in myself, which can be tough as not everything is funny when it first happens. The more you practice humor, though, the easier it is to laugh when things go wrong.

And things do go wrong. Here is an example. Years ago, I was a guest at a friend's house. I went to brush my teeth and realized I had forgotten my toothpaste. But, it was okay. I noticed a tube on the counter. I loaded up my toothbrush and began to brush, but noticed it did not have a minty-fresh taste. I picked up the tube to read what kind of strange toothpaste these people were using. To my surprise, it read Preparation H! Instead of getting mad, I activated my humor attitude and laughed.

The list just adds up for me... I have walked through the Atlanta airport with a very long piece of toilet paper hanging off the back of my pants, fallen down an escalator, gotten my leg stuck in a revolving door, and walked into a glass door like a bug hitting a windshield. While none of these experiences were initially funny to me, I was able, through my practice of lightening up and looking for the humor, to find the joy in each situation. I can now look back at any of these moments, think about the scenarios, and have a good laugh. That's the power of choosing to see the lighter side of events. You can reflect on them at any time and embrace the rewards.

A healthy attitude exists when we can laugh at ourselves and the crazy things we do, or find humor in what happens to us on a daily basis. It takes some practice, but is so worth it. Make humor a healthy habit and attitude in your life. The benefits: you will feel good and look good!

Humor can help you become more successful.

Think about Ronald Reagan. When he passed on and people acknowledged him, every person recognized two things about him – his leadership and his humor. His humor made him likeable. It broke the ice at meetings. His humor made people feel comfortable and eased the tension of stressful situations.

You don't have to be a comedian to incorporate good humor. Just choose to see the lighter side in situations and yourself. That's what Reagan did, and it added to his success.

Thomas Edison is praised for all his great inventions, but one of his greatest discoveries was in recognizing humor's effect on life and work. Edison had notebooks and notebooks filled with humor and jokes. He collected humor materials. He loved humor and shared it constantly with his staff and family. He discovered that a staff that laughs together works harder and more effectively together.

If you interview any successful leader, I bet that he or she will tell you that having a sense of humor is vital to great leadership. It helps keep things in perspective.

Humor can save you from terminal professionalism.

Do you work with people who might have a little terminal professionalism? They are uptight, negative, and not enjoyable to be around. Are you like this at all? Here is good way to test yourself: If you walk out of a room and hear celebrations or people praising God behind you, that might be a sign that you need to lighten up.

It's understandable that we have a lot on our plates at work and carry hefty responsibilities. Frustration can build when others are not working well with us. It's no doubt that the workplace has become a factory for burnout and stress-related illnesses. There are so many factors in the workplace that cause stress: deadlines, difficult people, sitting in traffic, phones ringing and the list goes on.

Did you know that more people drop dead on Monday before work than any other day of the week? It's safe to say, people are dying to go to work. If you don't enjoy what you do, it can make you uptight and negative.

So what can you do? You may not be able to control what's going on at work and what's going on around you, but you do have the power to choose how you respond to what's going on. Remember, your perception determines your responses.

Keeping your sense of humor will help you respond in healthy ways. It will relax you. You will breathe better and actually make your work more enjoyable. Humor is to our life what shocks are to a car. It helps us endure the bumps along the way.

Companies are recognizing the importance of wellness programs which incorporate mental components like humor. If the workplace is creating suppressed negativity, people will become unhealthy. Productivity will drop, creativity will decrease, service will be out to lunch all day, and teamwork will be sleeping on the couch in the break room. It is of value to the company and its future to keep morale up. Bottom line: When we feel good, we do well, and everyone wins.

How do you get and keep a positive sense of humor?

1. First, make the choice to lighten up. Give yourself permission to enjoy something funny. If you're not enjoying humor around you, you need to ask yourself why not? What limitation have you created in your mind that is serving as a road block to enjoying life more? Figure it out, and once you do, get over it... and fast. Hey... It's okay to have a good chuckle. Who cares if you look weird laughing and others see you? I am not saying to laugh at everything. Learn to laugh at the pure, the positive and the good. Don't laugh at the expense of others. Don't laugh at things that are distasteful. Laugh at effective and healthy humor.

2. Practice. You don't have to be a comedian to experience or communicate good humor; just choose to see the lighter side of situations and yourself. That's the starting point. Start off small, then gradually you will begin to see and experience more humor in your life.

3. Get around people who laugh. Laughter is contagious. It's always fun to be around someone who loves to laugh. Sooner or later, you will join in.

4. Collect humor material. Rent a funny movie and have a belly laugh. I like to cut out funny cartoons and post them up for all to see. My personal favorite humor-gathering activity is to collect hilarious stories and share them.

Here is one you might like:

Two elderly women were sitting on a bench waiting for a bus. The buses were running late, and a lot of time passed. Finally, one woman turned to the other and said, "You know, I've been sitting here so long, my butt fell asleep." The other woman turned to her and said, "I know. I heard it snoring."

Here are some humorous one-liners I collected from comedian Steven Wright:

1. If it's true that we are here to help others, then what exactly are others here for?

2. If Fed-Ex and UPS were to merge, would they call it FED UP?

3. What hair color do they put on a driver's license of a bald man?

4. If lawyers are disbarred and clergymen defrocked, doesn't it follow that electricians can be delighted, musicians denoted, cowboys deranged, models deposed, tree surgeons debarked, and dry cleaners depressed?

5. If people from Poland are called Poles, why aren't people from Holland called Holes?

6. Last night I played a blank tape at full blast. The mime next door went nuts.

7. If a cow laughed, would milk come out her nose?

Remember... **Humor is all around us.** You might be thinking *I have nothing to laugh at; there is nothing that's funny about me or anything in my life.* Sure there is, and in time, if you really look for it, you will see it. How do I know this? I am living proof. I battled depression for years, lost all joy for life, and forgot how to smile and laugh. Today, my life has been radically transformed by the power of humor. Sometimes I laugh so hard that I could almost pass out.

Attitude Kicker

*Using humor in the
workplace will:*

- Create positive human connections
- Lighten up meetings
- Bring down walls
- Unfold an attitude that makes you more likeable
- Cause people to serve better and sell more
- Open the door to prospective clients
- Create a spirit that will draw others as a source of energy and life
- Help staff maintain proper perspective
- Establish resiliency in challenging situations
- Instill self confidence in workers

Companies that cultivate humor in the workplace also cultivate people who will serve better, feel better, and work better. Some of us do need to lighten up, and the way we do that is by choosing to look at the lighter side of situations.

A Kick in the Attitude
Principle #9

Tame Your Tiger Or
It Will Eat You Alive

*Patience is the attitude of
self-control which involves
committing to think
before you respond.*

*It means responding in
a healthy way, instead of
reacting and creating regret.*

I remember sitting at Chicago O'Hare airport waiting for my plane to board. The gate agent came over the intercom and said, "Ladies and gentleman, I am very sorry, but there is a mechanical problem and there will be a three-hour delay."

You could hear the sighs, but the overall attitude was, I would rather wait for three hours for the plane to be fixed than be in the air and discover there is a problem. Well, right after the agent made the announcement, this little bald-headed guy walked up to the counter and let out fire! He screamed, "I WANT THIS PLANE TO FLY RIGHT NOW! BLAH, BLAH, BLAH!"

He was so angry that you would have thought his head was going to pop off. Now, let me ask a question, do you think he contributed positively to the situation, or let his negative emotions take control? It's pretty obvious. It was a situation that none of us could control. We could only control our responses. This guy, by losing control, did not benefit anyone.

Guess what? The plane did not take off any sooner due to his outbursts. The plane took off three hours later, just as the agent had predicted. This guy lost it for no good reason. He didn't benefit himself or the situation.

As you can see, losing control does not have healthy or positive benefits. Plus, when you lose control, you look pretty ridiculous. Have you ever seen a man have a temper tantrum and thought, "Boy, he sure looks good!" Hardly.

Now more than ever, we live in reactive times. Retaliating is easy. But it is to the betterment of your success and health to step back, think about your responses, and respond in a beneficial way. People of self-control respond in a way that benefits them and the situation. People of self-control use wisdom-power, not reactive-power.

Demonstrating self-control requires good emotional management. Let's say you have been stressed in some way and are fired up. Define some things that might calm you down. Use these soothing tools next time you get worked up. Listen to music, go for a walk, drink water, call someone, do anything to relieve the built-up negative emotions.

I am not telling you to suppress your negative emotions. You would turn into a volcano and eventually explode. I am only suggesting that you relieve the negative emotions in a more constructive way. I know that when I am stressed or on the brink of feeling negative, I hit the gym and walk on the treadmill for 30 minutes. I also have a few friends I can call, and when I do, they are ready to listen; but they also have a way of changing my attitude by interjecting some humor and encouragement. These actions diffuse the negative bomb that might be ticking inside me. I become balanced, healthy and in a better place to demonstrate self-control.

> **We may not have a choice about what situations we find ourselves in, but we do have a choice about the attitude we bring to the situation. And that attitude can change the overall experience and outcome.**

Here are a few ideas that will help you tame your tiger.

Practice patience.

What you practice in your life will surface in your life. Life requires us to respond. And there are moments when we feel less than patient.

Patience is eroded when we get worked up. People have been known to give themselves heart attacks because they got so worked up over a situation.

I remember once pulling out of a gas station, and in front of me was a huge big rig. Behind me was a very impatient driver who did not have the same vision that I had of what was going on in front of me. I could see the truck let someone pull out in front of him and I realized that if I pulled out, I would hit that person. It looked, however, like I was just sitting there not moving for no good reason. The car behind me got impatient, and tried to make a statement by pulling around me, getting into an accident as a result.

If you do not practice patience, you practice regret. You may say or do something you wish you could take back.

I love the story of the father who practiced patience with his daughter. He walked out to see her brushing the dog's teeth with his toothbrush. Instead of yelling or doing something regretful, he calmly said, "Honey, if you are going to use Daddy's toothbrush to brush the dog's teeth, you need to tell Daddy."

The little girl responded, "Okay, Daddy. But, what about all those other times?" We always have a choice in how we are going to respond.

Here are four elements that can push our buttons, which we often are forced to respond to on a daily basis:

1. Change
2. Challenges
3. The unexpected
4. Negative people

Years ago, I got hit with all four elements at once. I was riding a rollercoaster. I didn't know the guy sitting next to me, but I knew everyone behind me in the other carts. As we were climbing the first hill, the guy next to me got violently sick. It was a bad situation. He had food poisoning and everything in his body wanted to come out. I had a negative thought of pushing him out, but I didn't. I was encountering change, a challenge, the unexpected and a person who was creating a negative situation.

I didn't know what to do. I turned to my friends for support about the situation, but they just laughed at me. Finally it occurred to me: *There is nothing I can do about this.* I could freak out, but what good will that do? None.

We might not be able to control people or negative situations, but we can control the attitude that we bring to the situation, and that can change the overall outcome or result. So that is what I did.

There was nothing I could do to help this guy who was letting his lunch be known. I just put on an attitude of fun, put my hands in the air, and enjoyed the ride. But the ride turned out to be better than I thought. Remember all of my friends who were laughing at me? Well, the guy next to me could not keep his head down once the rollercoaster dropped. Let's just say that what goes around, comes around. It was a funny sight to behold.

You might think this is a gross story, but let me ask you a question: Did I ask for this to happen? No. Do I have to deal with it? Yes. We are all going to find ourselves in situations that we did not ask to be in. *The question is, how will you respond? Will you make the situation better or worse?*

When life throws you a challenging situation to which you have to respond, you need to ask yourself these questions:

"By the way I respond,…"

Will I make this situation worse?
Or
Will I make this situation better?

<u>Let it go and choose to make every situation better.</u>

This is your choice every time. A part of you may want to make it worse, because that's how you feel at the moment; but in the end you will hurt yourself and others.

This awareness has opened my mind to letting go, thinking it out, and responding to situations in a better way. The key is that we have to humble ourselves and choose to make the scenario better. One way to do that is by choosing to let it go. Another method is to step away from the situation for a bit before we respond. The reason we are told to count to 10 in tense situations is that counting is a simple way to separate our minds from the situation, allowing ourselves to diffuse the bomb in our minds.

You have to get separated or you will go mad and become reactive. Your thoughts will turn destructive and force you to take a regretful action. You will never respond in the right way when you have a hot head. Do something to cool down.

A good way to get calm, cool and relaxed, and to a place where your thinking is better is to renew your mind and body. Get recharged. If you are tired, stressed or hungry and you encounter a change, challenge, something unexpected or a negative person, you may not respond in the best of ways. You may just need to rest your mind and body for a bit. Take time to think it out.

I am not saying to never get mad. Things will happen and we will get upset. It's okay to be angry about something, but don't let the emotions of your wrath rule your actions and words.

Attitude Kicker

Remember that you can't take away something you say to someone when you are angry. You may think someone deserves a piece of your mind, but words can hurt not only who you deliver them to, but also yourself. If you say harmful things to someone else, most likely they will then harbor anger towards you. See how the cycle gets even more vicious? Instead, divert your anger to a journal, a counselor, or the gym until you can deliver it in a manner that won't abuse those around you.

Once it diffuses, you also might realize that the other person wasn't so in the wrong after all. Or you might decide that you are better off walking away from the situation and spending your energy on constructive tasks.

A Kick in the Attitude Principle #10

Be and Do What You Say

*The final forming of a
person's character lies
in their own hands.*

Anne Frank

A minister got on the public train system to go to his office downtown. He noticed that after he bought his ticket, the cashier attendant gave him back way too much money in change. As the minister rode to his office, thoughts danced in his mind about all the things he could do with the extra money. He thought this was a good thing, because times were tough. He even justified it as a gift from God: Nobody will miss it, and plus, I am good person. I can do something worthwhile with it.

But it continued to drive him nuts all day, to the point where he had to leave the office to return the money. When he showed up to give the money back, he said, "Young man, I am sorry but you gave me back way too much change this morning."

The young man smiled and said, "No I didn't. Yesterday I came to visit your church and you preached on character and integrity. I just wanted to see if you were for real!"

Character is doing what is right. Integrity is good character in action. Character is developed from what we do over and over and over and over and over. To create a healthy and rock-solid character, we need to develop healthy habits by repetitively practicing what is right.

The temptation to do the wrong thing will always pop up in front of you. What will do you do?

I remember walking through a hallway at a university which for some reason was full of pianos – around 20 of them. In front of the pianos was a sign, "Do not touch or play the pianos or there will be consequences to pay."

It was a strict sign; you got the idea they didn't want you touching these very expensive instruments. As I walked past each one, it took every urge in me not to reach down and hit a few bars. I wanted to, but I had self-control and avoided it.

There was a girl in front of me, however, who fell to the temptation. She reached down and played a few notes, and just then some crazy piano guy screamed at her and chased her down the hallway.

Whether someone is watching or not, it's ultimately up to you to choose what you will do. Having a solid character is about being responsible. It's not about being popular; it involves doing what is right. Character is not defined by your looks or anything on your outside. It is the core of what you stand for, will do in tough situations, and how you respond to life – it is who you are.

You can fool others some of the time, but you cannot fool yourself. You have to live with your character. And you are the one who will reap its largest rewards. If you are doing what you say you will and putting integrity into action, you don't have to look over your shoulder, cover your tracks or worry about a lack of character coming back to bite you.

Ask yourself this, can people trust you at your word? Will you really do what you say? If a camera were on you all the time for the world to watch, like in the movie "The Truman Show," how would your life look? The key to a having a solid character lies in knowing when it needs work, even if just fine tuning. Take a moment and define the values and morals that you will stand on and won't cross no matter what. The best way to think about this is to ask yourself what five traits would everyone who knows you use to define your character? Or what five traits would you like them to use? Honesty? Loyalty? Kindness? Sincerity? Responsibility? Humility?

Once you define your character, or the character you strive to have, then walk in it. Practice it every day... in both the little and big things.

Here are a few character-building points:

Practice integrity.

A short time ago, as I was walking off the airplane, I passed a seat upon which someone had left a Mont blanc pen. I am aware that Mont blanc pens are very nice and expensive. I was the last passenger off the plane, so nobody would have known if I had kept it or not. I could have justified that I really needed a nice pen. Maybe it was meant to be. The universe was giving back to me in the form of an expensive pen.

Nothing could be further from the truth. Because I make an effort to practice what I preach and live what I have defined, it wasn't hard to turn it in so the owner could retrieve it (well, maybe it was a little bit hard!).

Life will always present you with the opportunity to practice integrity. You likely really appreciate the value of integrity when it's given to you from someone else, so why not give it in return?

A few months back, I left my wallet in the grocery cart at Costco. I had close to $300 cash in there, and all of my credit cards. It didn't occur to me until five hours later. I thought, surely someone took it. By chance, I called Costco and they informed me that a woman and her daughter had returned it to the store. Ahhhh… relief.

You can feel the value of good character when something like this happens to you. Good character is knowing and abiding by the golden rule: do unto others as you would have done to you. A solid character counts for everything.

Do what you say you will do.

If you make a promise, fulfill it. And if you break it, don't create an excuse. Own it. Let your yes be yes and your no be no. Let your word be your bond.

Respect others.

Respecting others requires not talking about them behind their back. It involves not trying to take advantage of them. It includes respecting their background, race, and religion, realizing that we are all unique.

Own your mistakes.

One of my biggest pet peeves is when someone makes a mistake, but doesn't have the fortitude to own it. He or she takes up more energy and time to find someone or something to blame than would likely be spent making the situation right. My encouragement is that if you make a mistake, own it, admit it, fix it if you can, and move on.

Deal with let-downs.

Nothing breaks the heart faster than being let down by someone you trust. I have learned that words mean very little, but actions mean everything. A part of me thought about listing everyone – the names, the companies – that have taken advantage, deceived, lied, obtained money that was not properly earned, or demonstrated unethical practices in working with me. I have a good-sized list, but I am reminded of the wisdom of Jim Rohn, "Successful people don't spend time getting even; they focus on getting ahead."

We can't control the practice of ethics – doing what is right – in others. I've had people say exactly what I wanted to hear, only to have their actions not match their words. The result of working or developing relationships with people who lack integrity is that people get hurt. People lose money. When on the receiving end of someone's lack of integrity, it's hard to trust again.

But no matter the size of your pain, it is wasted energy to try and get even or show someone up. Revenge often ends up costing you more.

Practice forgiveness.

This may be the hardest action of all, but the value of forgiveness is ironically for you, not for the person you are forgiving. You need to find and make the peace, lest whatever happened eat you up on the inside for a long time.

Sometimes people close to us will make little mistakes that let us down. We need to find the courage to forgive and not carry the weight of what happened. If there is a way to resolve the situation in a healthy way, then do that.

Today, there are many studies on forgiveness, which point to the fact that those who forgive are healthier. What more reason do you need?

This is not to say that there is never recourse for setting things right with someone. If something is beyond your control, for example, and true harm has been caused, I believe that it is okay to consider action, even involving the justice system. Justice will find a way of catching up to those who are truly unethical and hurtful – for every action, there is a consequence, and the snake eventually will bite those who do wrong. You may not see it, but it will happen. But if you do sue, try to keep your heart in a forgiving place.

If you have ever been let down and think, "I can never trust again," I want to let you know that it is okay to trust again. Not everyone is out to get you, and you will find that not everyone will let you down. Practice caution, but don't hide under a rock. Each situation of let-down teaches you to become wiser. Carry the discernment with you to situations in your future.

If you have been bit by someone's lack of integrity, my encouragement is:

1. Be a person of integrity at all times, even when you are tempted to seek revenge.
2. Be ethical – do what is right.
3. Respond with good wisdom – seek counsel and find options in how to respond. You don't want to stir a fire.
4. Let go, get over it, and move on.
5. Don't react with feelings. We tend to want to explode first – but rather act with principle, which I have shared in the above.

Attitude Kicker

If you aren't sure how to act in a given situation, make a list of the things that you value most in life. List not only the material things, but the traits you don't ever want to divert from. Maybe it is your family, or your health, or honesty. Then anytime you get angry or agitated, or you aren't sure which road to go down, refer to the list of values, and make sure your actions will support rather than compromise those things.

In time, acting on your values will get easier, and you may not need to reference the list so often. You will also see your life unfold in ways that make you feel good inside.

Kick in the Attitude Principle #11

You Ain't No Good If You're All Spent

And in the end, it's not the years in your life that count. It's the life in your years.

Abraham Lincoln

Years ago, I decided to go for a jog. I wanted to get out and get some fresh air and exercise. I had been putting it off all day due to my very long to-do list. I had phone calls to make, projects to finish, and was feeling the stress. It was hitting me in every direction. I could feel my mood shifting to a negative one. I had such a pounding headache. I knew that I had been on the same crazy schedule for weeks and my body was about to crash.

As I started jogging, I played in my mind all the daily activities and allowed myself to get even more stressed. CRACK! My ankle twisted. I fell to the ground and lay there in pain. Suddenly, I was no longer thinking about my to-do list, the phone calls, or what was stressing me out. All those things vanished from my mind just like that. The only thing that mattered was my ankle.

I was about a mile from home and knew that I could not walk that far. A farmer driving by saw me lying there on the side of the road and offered me a ride home. When I got home, I plopped right down on the couch with a bag of ice. The situation forced me to relax.

Later, I went to the doctor to get my ankle checked. He told me I had a sprain and needed to ice it, stay off of it, and relax.

There was a word I was not used to hearing: relax. How do you do that? My mind and body were not yet trained for such a thing. I was a magnet for stress and experiencing the effects of it physically and emotionally. My injury forced me to sit on the couch and do nothing. Well, not nothing, it forced me to relax. Once I gave in, my ankle got better, my energy level increased, my mood improved, and my spirit lifted. All thanks to a little relaxation.

One of the hardest life lessons to grasp is to take adequate time to renew ourselves, to slow down and let go in order to get back to a place of strength. It's hard to live your best if you are running on fumes. We need time to rest, relax, think, reflect, and let go. If we don't take the time to release, our stress will begin to manifest itself in negative ways physically and emotionally.

The key to healthy living is not in waiting to be forced to rest, but in planning it with purpose. And it's not easy. We live in times when we practice stress, rather than renewal, on a daily basis. We have to be aware of how harmful too much unmanaged stress is and why renewing ourselves can be crucial in creating reserves to last us through.

If I asked you to stand on one leg for a few minutes, I bet you could do it. But what if I asked you to stand on one leg for a few hours? Eventually, you would fall over from exhaustion. At first, the stress of standing on one leg would be manageable, but the longer you stood there, the more unbearable the strain would become, causing you to fall.

We can only do so much of what we do without running into burnout. The stress can build to a place where we are no longer any good for ourselves, relationships or work.

It's important to recognize the signs of needing renewal. Here are just a few: constant fatigue, moodiness, snapping, rage, frustration, depression, tense neck muscles, forgetfulness, headaches, and a spike in weight gain or loss. While these can all be symptoms for a lot of other underlying issues, in basic terms they spell out an overly stressed person whose mind and body needs some rest. Many of these factors can put us at a higher risk of heart disease. Plus, if we are running on fumes, our minds become magnets for negative thinking. We might carry around unnecessary thoughts that get blown out of proportion. We might be more prone to saying and doing something regretful. A lack of energy can feed your tiger, as we discussed in the last chapter.

The lesson of needing to recharge ourselves is something we can see all around us. Think of your cell phone. I have to recharge mine every night when I get ready for bed. What about when your kids get cranky? Our first thought is, *this kid needs a nap.* Taking a necessary rest is a lesson we must grasp and apply to our lifestyle, no matter what we do.

What are the benefits to recharging yourself?

As I have mentioned in this book over and over, life gets better when we get better. We make our life better when we operate from our best place – a place of strength and energy. In order to do that, we have to recharge ourselves. The benefits are many... We are more productive. We take care of ourselves more effectively. The experiences we create for others are of a higher quality. Our relationships improve. Our passion and enthusiasm are rekindled. We no longer carry around unmanaged stress that causes us to drag, but we are energized and ready to get the best out of ourselves and life.

Here are a few ideas to help recharge yourself.

Go for a walk.

As you walk, let go of your day. Be in the moment.

Take a nap.

Thomas Edison used to have a cot in his office so he could take 10 minute naps to get recharged. Rest for 10 to 20 minutes to get a quick recharge.

Get out of town.

Plan a getaway… often. Not just once a year, but maybe once every few months. It doesn't have to be long. Just a few days will do wonders. I personally enjoy getting away and fishing. It always revitalizes me when I can sit on the beach and just watch the sunset and crashing waves.

Getting out of town can help separate you from your world. And that's key to recharging yourself. There will always be things to get done – projects, deadlines, and theunexpected – but in order to face them with strength, you have to be at your best. Sometimes finding your best requires losing your worries in a fresh environment for a short time.

Do nothing.

Sometimes I do nothing and I get a lot out of it. I may just watch TV, sit on my porch, take a two-hour nap, or putter around. There are times when if you called me and asked, "What are you doing?" I would tell you, "Nothing, and loving it." Really, it's just me resting, and not thinking about work, bills, projects, etc…

Go for a spa treatment.

Pamper yourself with a massage. Doing this can rid your muscles of toxins that have built up due to stress.

Here is a list of other things you can do to recharge yourself:

- Call and talk with a good friend.
- Go watch a good movie.
- Take a few deep breaths.
- Exercise.
- Eat something healthy.
- Read a good book.
- Take a shower or bath.
- Listen to some good tunes.
- Do some art.
- Pray.

Make recharging your emotional and physical batteries a priority. To be at your best, you have to be active about it. We are going to encounter stress on a daily basis, and too much of it left unmanaged can hurt us. If you try to get up the mountain on fumes, you are not going to make it. You won't be happy, and life will seem like a drag. So make the choice to slow down, let go and get renewed. When you do, you will always come face to face with your best self.

Attitude Kicker

Did you know that even professional athletes have periods of rest? You can't go forever. Do you have unspent vacation time that has been accruing for years? Spend it now. I'm not encouraging you to be lazy, but find a balance in your life that allows you to appreciate just being alive.

Kick In the Attitude Principle #12

Make Footprints, Not Butt Prints

If you want to touch the past... touch a rock.

If you want to touch the present... touch a rose.

If you want to touch the future... touch a life.

Unknown

If there is one action I know of that restores an eminent energy of hope and enthusiasm into our very existence, it is when we reach out to make a difference. It's stepping out and making an attitude contribution of kindness, care, encouragement and love. That's the core of what creating a legacy is all about. It involves bringing the greatness of who you are to someone who needs it. Empowering ourselves starts by reaching out to empower others. What we send out really does return to us multiplied. Proverbs 11:25 says, "He who refreshes others will himself be refreshed."

Sometimes it can be so easy to get discouraged in our efforts to make a difference. But the question you have to ask yourself is this: What will your legacy be? What do you want it to be? What will others remember of you when you are gone? What actions did you take to make someone's day or life better, or bigger? We will all be remembered for something, so why not be remembered in a way that includes a legacy?

That's one of the reasons why I am writing this book. I want it to enrich the lives of others – yours at this time, and those who read it when I am gone.

We all have something to give.

We all showed up with a unique and special gift in life. It's the ability to make a difference in the lives of others. Making such a difference can happen in such a simple act as getting a friend who is having a bad day a Happy Meal from McDonalds. When they ask you why you got it for them, you can say, "If you eat it, it will make you happy. So, I got you four of them."

I once had someone in my audience put this into practice. He was at Wal-Mart, and the cashier was very rude to him. We always have a choice when we encounter a negative attitude. We can simply move on, or we can stop and use our difference-making abilities to draw out the best in others.

On the surface, you may encounter a negative and defeating attitude in someone else, but if you seek out the person's best, you can find it. You can take on the attitude of Luke Skywalker in Return of the Jedi, when he kept telling his father, Darth Vader, "I know there is good in you, Father."

There is good in all of us, and sometimes it gets covered up by hard times, frustrating co-workers, a situation at home – who knows. But, as a difference maker, you have the ability to resurface someone's best.

So getting back to the story, this guy and his wife went to McDonalds to buy this cashier from Wal-Mart a Happy Meal. The wife wanted to rant about his rudeness to the manager, but the husband said, "Let's just see what happens." They got back in line, and when they stepped up, the cashier was still rude.

They placed the Happy Meal down, and the cashier looked at them asking, "What's this?"

"It's a Happy Meal. You looked like you could use one tonight. If you eat it, it will make you happy."

The cashier about melted. His hard looking face softened. His shoulders dropped and the tension dissolved. He smiled, and with tears in his eyes, said, "I am sorry if I treated you badly. It's been a hard day. Nobody has ever done anything like this for me before. Thank you."

This fellow told me that every time he goes to Wal-Mart now and checks out, that guy smiles and treats him with the best he has.

> *Don't let discouragement keep you from writing your legacy in life.*

We all have something to give that can make a difference. Each of us can lend a hand, give a hug, give of our time, make a phone call, get involved, clean toilets, pray with someone…

Don't keep your music and gifts locked up; open up and let the colors of who you are and what you have to give touch the life of another. Take a moment to think about what you have to offer that will make a positive impression in time. Making a difference doesn't take much. It only requires an attitude of willingness to step out, step up and step forth to make a difference. Think about something amazing someone did for you. Didn't it feel great and touch your heart? Why not do that for someone else?

Let me share a simple yet profound statement about creating a legacy. In life, we will either make footprints or butt prints in the sands of time. Making footprints means you tried, got up, dumped the excuses, used what you had, and best of all, made a positive impression in time with the gift of who you are.

Making butt prints means you did just the opposite. You sat life out.

The difference is that one has you looking back saying, "I am glad I did," while the other has you saying, "I wish I had." Nobody wants to look back and feast on thoughts of regret. We are all valuable with incredible gifts ripe for making an impact. We simply must step out and use them, rather than sit down and ride this life out.

I have been on the receiving end of someone else's graciousness. The first Christmas after my parents divorced, it was just me, my two brothers and mom. We didn't have much money, yet someone got us a box of food for the holidays. And while it was humbling to accept, we did. I remember my mom's tears, and how thankful she was that someone had lent a helping hand during such a hard time. Someone made footprints on my life that day.

The portrait of a footprint maker.

Most called him Richard Albertson, but for the short time that I knew him, I called him Gramps. My grandpa was a giant, both in physical stature and with his attitude. He could make almost anyone smile, which was his special gift.

I have seemingly small memories of him that fill me with great warmth... For example, whenever you drove in his old red pickup truck, it did not matter who you were, he would get you to sing with him, "You are my sunshine... my only sunshine, you make me happy when skies are gray... how much I miss you, so please don't take my sunshine away." What an impact that had on the attitude of those around him. As corny as it seemed at the time, his silly ways put a smile on our faces and made us feel really good!

Gramps had his own special way with people. He had a touch of joy that he left in people's hearts. He always seemed ready to go the extra mile to help others. If it were in his capacity, he would do whatever he could for you. That was his nature, or one that he acquired over his years of learning and life lessons. Everywhere I went with him, it seemed like everyone knew him, and Gramps always had a kind word to offer. My grandpa was very approachable. He could talk to strangers like he'd known them for years. He always expressed interest in people.

Gramps was a nice guy, but I do remember that if we ever got out of line, he would let us know it, exclaiming, "Holy buckets!" I will always remember him as the giant who could touch the ceiling with his hands, play the organ and get us dancing, take us fishing in a heartbeat, and make us feel like he simply loved spending time with us. He didn't have a big organization that was out to change the world, he didn't go speak to large groups, and he didn't even have that much money to give. But what he did have, he used and shared, and that was plenty to make a difference – a lesson we can all live by. He, like all of us, had a uniqueness within him, an impression to leave in the world... He left footprints in the sand... not butt prints.

In 1989, my grandpa passed away due to lung cancer. He was sick for a long time, and it broke my heart to see such a dear man breathing from an oxygen tank. In his last days, I remember seeing this giant of a man looking worn out with very little life left in him. I learned how priceless our time is here with others; it's but a flicker!

My grandfather's death was my first real experience of losing someone close. At his funeral, many people showed up – some I knew and many I did not. I listened to people tell stories about Gramps and some of the audience even engaged in laughter. Some wore expressions of happiness while others remembered him in tears. My grandpa touched many lives with who he was, the way he lived, and what he gave.

Watching all this made me realize something about life. When people laugh, cheer, celebrate, give thanks, or remember you in tears at your funeral, it is not because you are gone, but because you have touched their lives with the greatness of who you are. When you touch other people's lives, life seems to give you back rewards beyond words, beyond money, and almost always beyond expression. The reward goes to the treasure chest in our hearts. It makes footprints.

Get Involved.

Years ago, I wanted to get involved with a group called Fellowship of Christian Athletes through an internship at a summer camp in Marshall, Indiana. What I had in mind and what they had planned, however, were two different agendas. They wanted me to clean dishes and bathrooms in all the cabins. After one day of cleaning bathrooms, I reevaluated my passion to make a difference that summer. I didn't want to clean toilets. I wanted to be amongst the people to talk and engage in what I considered meaningful activities.

I was about ready to quit, when the camp director opened my eyes to what it really meant to make a difference. My attitude had been wrong. As a result, I was seeing the worst in the situation. He told me point blank, "If you don't clean those bathrooms, then who will? And if you only do an average, get-by job, then does that really make a difference?"

The lesson in this for me was that making a difference can start by something as seemingly small as picking up a piece of trash from the ground, or filling in where it's needed most. And no, these may not always be the most glamorous jobs, but if you have a heart to make a difference, then you will put on the right attitude that gets the task done well.

I did just that. I got passionate about cleaning the bathrooms. In fact, I started cleaning the bathrooms with the expectation that whoever used them would feel the difference. I put up positive quotes on the mirrors and did a job that had my supervisor wanting to hire me full time. The experience changed my life, and altered my outlook on what it really meant to make a difference and create a legacy.

Attitude Kicker

Think right now about someone who made a big difference in your life. Was it someone famous, or even super successful? Maybe, but I doubt it was their fame or success that made the difference. It was probably something small they did to reach out to you, which made a huge difference. So remember, you may touch lives and leave your mark with the smallest remark or gesture. You don't have to be famous or wealthy to touch someone's life, to leave a lasting impression.

A Kick in the Attitude Principle #13

Never Give Up!

One word or a pleasing smile is often enough to raise up a saddened and wounded soul.

St Teresa of Lisieux

In the beginning of my speaking career I had the great opportunity to sit down to lunch with Peter Lowe. Peter is an example of someone who didn't give up, and therefore achieved his dreams. He began with small motivational seminars and at his first event, got a less than great showing. However, he was thrilled that his family showed up. He didn't give up and eventually began to host huge motivational meetings – filling arenas with thousands of people.

I was honored to have him bestow his wisdom and experience onto me, and the first thing he said as we sat down was something like, "Sam, all I can tell you is don't give up. Don't give up."

It's okay to rest, but don't stop and give up on your dreams. If one dream dies, dream a new one. Is it easy? Not at all. Is it possible? Yes! History has already proven as much. Now, just prove it to yourself. Be your own inspirational story.

How many times has life thrown a curve ball that makes us think, I want to give up, throw in the towel, go to sleep and not wake up? I personally have walked in such shoes. But the encouragement of those around me has pushed me to keep up the run until the finish line is crossed. Soak up all the encouragement you can. It's fuel for your dream's journey.

Relationships that offer encouragement are so valuable and need to be treasured. We need to be reminded that we can make it.

But even without others to tell us so, we need to remember that we can make it over, under, around or through whatever we are experiencing.

Surround yourself with encouragers.

Life would be nearly impossible if we had to journey through it alone. We need to find strength in each other.

Dr. Mike Murdock says, "People will either increase us or decrease us." We need to surround ourselves with "increase" people – people who love us, encourage us, help us and give us wisdom.

Take an inventory of those who increase you. Value that support. Don't take it for granted – ever! There are some people who come into our lives and do things we can never repay them for. If we cannot directly give them thanks, then we can pass along their gifts by living right, thinking right, doing right and living the best we can.

Be an encourager.

If you feel like you don't have anyone in your life, then go out and be a support to someone. "He who refreshes others, will himself be refreshed." - Pr 11:25. Whatever you send out, it will come back. If you need love, encouragement and support, then give it first, and it will return to you in ways that you cannot even possibly imagine!

Let me close with this... Whatever season you are going through right now, know this truth, "You can make it."

99.9% of challenges come without warning.

In 1990, my family's town was literally wiped off the map by a microburst. A microburst is a huge storm wherein the sky opens up and air is pushed down. When it hits the ground, it spreads like a tornado and destroys.

It started as a mildly warm August afternoon, with no indication of an upcoming storm. The sky looked normal. I was putting on my tennis shoes in order to head to the park to play some basketball before I had to pick my mom up from work.

After I walked upstairs and looked outside, however, I saw that the sky had changed suddenly and the wind had picked up to a frightening degree. Rain shortly turned to hail the size of golf balls, pelting the house. I wasn't sure what was going on, but within two minutes, our house began to shake and rumble.

I was freaked out as I was home alone. The noise was deafening, and the only thing I could do was flip our wooden couch over on top of me and pray.

Then, just like that, the storm was gone and the sun was back. When I walked outside, I saw something that would shock anyone's eyes. The house next to us and the entire neighborhood beyond it were completely destroyed. The storm had wiped away everything up to our house, but we were spared.

It was a day and half before they declared our town of Plainfield, Illinois, a federal disaster. Twenty-eight people lost their lives and thousands were injured in the tragedy. Many lost their homes. Our town looked like a bomb had hit it.

The storm had come without warning. There was no siren or breaking news announcing that it was on the way. And that's the way a lot of our challenges come. They don't set up appointments. They just come, leaving us feeling hopeless and helpless. In moments like these, we want to give up.

Over the years, I have embraced hundreds of stories from people who have sat in my audience, suffering from the latest storm: the divorce, the death, the cancer, the abuse, the job loss, the dysfunction, the depression and so much more. Each story leaves someone whose heart and spirit seems to be broken.

I think we all have experienced a painful broken

heart of some sort. And all I can say is we need each other. I love this saying, "The strength of the wolf is in the pack and the strength of the pack is in the wolf."

So here it is – believe these words - you can make it, whether or not you can hear the echoes of your encouragers. Don't give up or lose hope. Dr. Norman Vincent Peale once said, "The only people without problems are in cemeteries." I also remember one person telling me, "Nobody goes through life untouched."

We will all be touched in some way at some time. It's okay to feel the pain and look for the meaning in the experience, but don't stop living. This is your opportunity to have your life deepened in ways you may not yet be able to imagine, but remember this... It all starts with attitude.

Attitude Kicker

Imagine running a marathon, getting within a half mile of the finish, and deciding, "Well, that was pretty good, and I'm pretty darned tired. I think I'll stop now." You wouldn't do it, right? Don't give up. Your reward is just ahead.

Let's Wrap It Up... What Does a Kick in the Attitude Mean to You?

My goal in sharing this book with you has been to deepen your awareness of how dynamic your attitude is, what it can do for you and why it is so significant to every aspect of your life. My focus for you has been to stretch yourself to do more than simply try to be positive.

Take a moment to glance again at the 13 attitude traits listed below.

- **Courage**
- **Determination**
- **Perseverance**
- **Persistence**
- **Gratefulness**
- **Sense of Humor**
- **Patience**
- **Enthusiasm**
- **Faith**
- **Confidence**

- **Excellence**
- **Kindness**
- **Love**

While I may not have mentioned each of these traits specifically, they were all woven throughout the lessons in this book. And as I have come to understand, they are all vital components of a healthy attitude, and thus a healthy life.

But as you will notice, they only work wonders in our lives when we put them into action. If we desire to be profitable in our relationships and work, we must practice these traits until they become our own.

When we do take possession of our lives in this way, our world becomes limitless. By embracing the power of our attitude, we will truly experience a kick in our lives. That kick will not only get us through, but will expand our horizons, delivering us on golden wings.

Sometimes life has a way of knocking the kick out of us, and my sincere hope is that this book has restored or enhanced your kick and your best attitude, so that you have the courage and energy to go out there and capture what life has in store for you. My goal for you is not just to get by, but to live a life that is brimming with joy and promise – a life with a true kick! You are worth it!

I also hope that you will use this book and refer to it often on your journey through life. Some chapters will have more meaning than others during different moments of your life, but keep this book close and know that it's always here to put the kick back into your attitude!

Now, without further adieu, go and enjoy your kick!

Meet the author, Sam Glenn
The Authority on Attitude!™

Sam Glenn resides in Chicago, Illinois. He lives minutes from where they film *Oprah*, and dreams about the day he will be a guest on the show and jump on all the furniture like Tom Cruise did (well, okay, maybe not quite like that). Sam has become one of the most in-demand, premier inspirational and motivational keynote speakers in the country. This once night-time janitor who slept on borrowed floor space now invigorates audiences of every size and some as large as 75,000, with side-splitting humor, inspirational insights and candid simplicity. Sam Glenn is regarded as the nation's foremost Authority on Attitude™ and has written 17 books on the subject of Attitude and Peak Performance in life and the workplace. Sam is the Founder of *Attitude Digest* magazine, which targets senior level managers, and entrepreneurs who are looking to inspire their staff members. The magazine is motivational, insightful, and fun. Sam is a prominent and highly sought after inspirational speaker, and has recieved extensive recent press coverage (MSNBC, Associated Press, Fox Business, Chicago Tribune, WGN and over 1,000 newspapers nationwide). In Sam's free time, he enjoys eating and laughing with his family, fishing, making others look good on the golf course, rooting for the Minnesota Vikings, and making prank phone calls to his relatives in the late night hours.

Tell us what you thought about this book:
Email: Contact@everythingattitude.com

Sign up for Sam's Inspirational Quote of the Week:
Visit: EverythingAttitude.com

800-818-6378

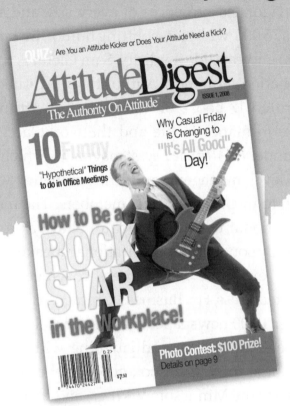